Sikhism

Date: 2/28/13

Sikhism

DORIS R. JAKOBSH

Dimensions of Asian Spirituality

UNIVERSITY OF HAWAI'I PRESS

Honolulu

DIMENSIONS OF ASIAN SPIRITUALITY

Henry Rosemont Jr., General Editor

This series makes available short but comprehensive works on specific Asian philosophical and religious schools of thought, works focused on a specific region, and works devoted to the full articulation of a concept central to one or more of Asia's spiritual traditions. Series volumes are written by distinguished scholars in the field who not only present their subject matter in historical context for the non-specialist reader, but also express their own views of the contemporary spiritual relevance of their subject matter for global citizens of the twenty-first century.

Library of Congress Cataloging-in-Publication Data

Jakobsh, Doris R.

Sikhism / Doris R. Jakobsh.

p. cm.— (Dimensions of Asian spirituality)

Includes bibliographical references and index.

ISBN 978-0-8248-3533-0 (hardcover : alk. paper) —

ISBN 978-0-8248-3601-6 (pbk. : alk. paper)

1. Sikhism. I. Title. II. Series: Dimensions of Asian spirituality.

BL2018.J35 2012

294.6—dc22

2011006891

University of Hawai'i Press books are printed on acid-free paper and meet the guidelines for permanence and durability of the Council on Library Resources.

Designed by Rich Hendel

Printed by Sheridan Books, Inc.

Contents

Editor's Preface

ABOUT THIS SERIES

The University of Hawai'i Press has long been noted for its scholarly publications in, and commitment to, the field of Asian studies. This series, Dimensions of Asian Spirituality, is in keeping with that commitment. It is a most appropriate time for such a series. A number of the world's religions—major and minor—originated in Asia, continue to influence significantly the lives of a third of the world's peoples, and should now be seen as global in scope, reach, and impact, with rich and varied resources for every citizen of the twenty-first century to explore.

Religion is at the heart of every culture. To be sure, the members of every culture have also been influenced by climate, geology, and the consequent patterns of economic activity they have developed for the production and distribution of goods. Only a minimal knowledge of physical geography is necessary to understand why African sculptors largely employed wood as their medium while their Italian Renaissance equivalents worked with marble. But while necessary for understanding cultures—not least our own—matters of geography and economics will not be sufficient: Marble is also found in China, yet the Chinese sculptor carved a bodhisattva, not a pietà, from his block.

In the same way, a mosque, synagogue, cathedral, stupa, and pagoda may be equally beautiful, but they are beautiful in different ways, and the differences cannot be accounted for merely on the basis of the materials used in their construction. Their beauty, their ability to inspire awe and to invite contemplation, rests largely on the religious view of the world—and the place of human beings in that world—that is expressed in their architecture. The spiritual dimensions of a culture are reflected significantly not only in art and architecture, but in music, myths, poetry, rituals, customs, and patterns of social behavior as well. Therefore it follows that if we wish to understand why and how members of other cultures live as they do, we must understand the religious beliefs and practices to which they adhere.

In the first instance, such understanding of the "other" leads to tolerance, which is surely a good thing. Much of the pain and suffering in the world today is attributable to intolerance, a fear and hatred of those who look, think, and act differently. But as technological changes in communication, production, and transportation shrink the world, more and more people must confront the fact of human diversity in multiply diverse forms—both between and within nations—and hence there is a growing need to go beyond mere tolerance of difference to an appreciation and celebration of it. Tolerance alone cannot contribute substantively to making the world a better— and sustainable—place for human beings to live, the evils attendant on intolerance notwithstanding and not to be diminished. But in an important sense, mere tolerance is easy because it is passive: I can fully respect your right to believe and worship as you wish, associate with whomever, and say what you will, simply by ignoring you; you assuredly have a right to speak, but not to make me listen.

Yet for most of us who live in economically developed societies, or are among the affluent in developing nations, tolerance is not enough. Ignoring the poverty, disease, and gross inequalities that afflict fully a third of the human race will only exacerbate, not alleviate, the conditions responsible for the misery that generates the violence becoming ever more commonplace throughout the world today. That violence will cease only when the more fortunate among the peoples of the world become active, take up the plight of the less fortunate, and resolve to create and maintain a more just world, a resolve that requires a full appreciation of the co-humanity of everyone, significant differences in religious beliefs and practices notwithstanding.

Such appreciation should not, of course, oblige everyone to endorse all of the beliefs and practices within their own faith. A growing number of Catholics, for instance, support changes in church practice: a married clergy, the ordination of women, recognition of rights for gays and lesbians, and full reproductive rights for women. Yet they remain Catholics, believing that the tenets of their faith have the conceptual resources to bring about and justify these changes.

In the same way, we can also believe—as a number of Muslim women do—that the Quran and other Islamic theological writings contain the conceptual resources to overcome the inferior status of women in some Muslim countries. And indeed we can believe that every spiritual tradition has within it the resources to counter older practices inimical to the full flourishing of all the faithful—and of the faithful of other traditions as well.

Another reason to go beyond mere tolerance to appreciation and celebration of the many and varied forms of spiritual expression is virtually a truism: the more we look through a window on another culture's beliefs and practices, the more it becomes a mirror of our own (even for those who follow no religious tradition). We must look carefully and charitably, however, else the reflections become distorted. When studying other religions, most people are inclined to focus on cosmological and ontological questions, asking, What do these people believe about how the world came to be and is, and where is it heading? Do they believe in ghosts? Immortal souls? A creator god?

Answering these and related metaphysical questions is of course necessary for understanding and appreciating the specific forms and content of the art, music, architecture, rituals, and traditions inspired by the specific religion under study. But the sensitive—and sensible—student will bracket the further question of whether the metaphysical pronouncements are literally true; we must attend carefully to the metaphysics (and theologies) of the religions we study, but questions of their literal truth should be set aside to concentrate on a different question: How could a thoughtful, thoroughly decent human being subscribe to and follow these beliefs and attendant practices?

Studied in this light, we may come to see and appreciate how each religious tradition provides a coherent account of a world not fully amenable to human manipulation, nor perhaps even to full human understanding. The metaphysical pronouncements of the world's religions of course differ measurably from faith to faith, and each has had a significant influence on the physical expressions of the respective faith in synagogues, stupas, mosques, pagodas, and cathedrals. Despite these differences between the buildings, however, the careful and sensitive observer can see the spiritual dimensions of human life that these sacred structures share and express, and in the same way we can come to see and appreciate the common spiritual dimensions of each religion's differing metaphysics and theology: While the several traditions give different answers to the question of the meaning *of* life, they provide a multiplicity of guidelines and spiritual disciplines to enable everyone to find meaning *in* life, in this world. By plumbing the spiritual depths of other religious traditions, then, we may come to more deeply explore the spiritual resources of our own, and at the same time diminish the otherness of the other and create a more peaceable and just world, in which everyone can find meaning in their all-too-human lives.

ABOUT THIS BOOK

Although Sikhism recently replaced Judaism as the world's fifth largest religion, relatively few people outside the faith know of its origins and later history, and probably even less about its metaphysics, ethics, rituals, and practices. Yet in 2004 the world's largest democracy elected the first Sikh to become head of a national government when Manmohan Singh became India's fourteenth prime minister. It is a small but dynamic faith and, like Judaism, has had influence greater than its numbers would suggest, especially for and on the Asian continent. For these and many more reasons, Doris Jakobsh's *Sikhism* is a most welcome addition to the Dimensions of Asian Spirituality series.

Again like the Jewish people in many respects, Sikhs may be said to be a "people of the book," in that their sacred scriptures and concern for their own history have always been central to the expression of their faith. Thus Jakobsh appropriately opens her work with a brief account of the writings of the ten gurus, beginning with the first and founder of the religion, Guru Nanak, in the fifteenth century, and then goes on to sketch his life and ideas and those of his successors.

Collectively the texts of the gurus are known as the Guru Granth Sahib, with the specific name Dasam Granth referring to the writings of the final guru in the pantheon, Guru Gobind Singh (d. 1708). What is perhaps most remarkable about the Guru Granth Sahib is that it is for the most part to be taken as hymns, to be sung as a sacrament and also to bring the singer closer in harmony with Akal Purakh, translated as "Eternal Being," an expression not devoid of anthropomorphic overtones for Sikhs but more frequently linked to what we would describe in English as the infinite, the eternal, or simply as the All There Is. Or as Jakobsh herself states it,

> In essence, then, Sikh scripture is revelatory, communicated by the Sikh gurus and other enlightened individuals as timeless correspondence between Akal Purakh and humanity. (p. 2)

After a meditation on the significance of studying and writing about history, Jakobsh goes on in later chapters to provide one for Sikhism, followed by accounts of the extent to which Sikhs are similar to, but distinct from, their Hindu and Muslim counterparts in South Asia; Sikh rituals, practices, and celebrations; the status of women in the Sikh religion; Sikhs as warriors; Sikhs in the diaspora; and concluding with reflections on the Sikh future.

Through all these topics Jakobsh weaves the musicality so fundamental to the Sikh way of life, which for them seems to be even more important than language for communicating a sense of the oneness of the infinite and the eternal, thereby enabling practitioners to commune with, and perhaps come to feel union with Akal Purakh, the Divine, the Eternal One.

And to link the divine with the worldly, she also repeatedly returns to describe and discuss the holiest of the holy sites of Sikhism, the Golden Temple of Amritsar, which I believe every reader of *Sikhism* will thereafter place alongside the Taj Mahal at the top of their must-see list for India. Even more in the world of the profane, and on an entirely different note, technologically sophisticated readers will welcome the many Web and other electronic resources Jakobsh has added to her bibliography of suggested readings in the final section of the work.

In sum, *Sikhism* proffers a clear and concise account of the Sikh religious tradition, with respect to both its sacred and secular dimensions, attentive to the historical past, the present, and its possible future in Asia and in the West; it is therefore another splendid addition to the Dimensions of Asian Spirituality series of the University of Hawai'i Press.

HENRY ROSEMONT JR.
NEWPORT, RHODE ISLAND

Acknowledgments

Let me begin by thanking Henry Rosemont for his kind invitation to contribute to the Dimensions of Asian Spirituality series, an invitation that came with clearly defined boundaries, equally clear expectations of the series as a whole, alongside concise guidelines accompanying each volume in the series. The writing of introductory texts of any form can be fraught with discontent as one is forced to mindfully grapple with what stays and what goes—in other words, extracting the supplementary from the essential, never an easy task when writing about religion and sacred truths. Henry's patient counsel in matters of organization, form, and tone, all the while leaving the content of the material to each contributor, has led, I believe, to a series holding fast to the ideals of rigorous scholarship while allowing for a connection between the writer and reader of each volume. My thanks also to Patricia Crosby and the rest of the editorial team at the University of Hawai'i Press for assistance and kind patience throughout the writing and publishing process.

Humble gratitude goes out to my students at the University of Waterloo, most particularly to those in my Sikhism courses. Addressing their assumptions, questions, and unwillingness to settle for easy answers, based largely on their own experiences in organized religions, played an integral role in shaping my approach in the writing of this volume. Clearly, learning and teaching about Sikhism, or any other religion, mean going beyond neat and tidy categories that allow for neat and tidy conclusions.

I am indebted to my colleagues and friends Eleanor Nesbitt, Pashaura Singh, Michael Hawley, and Himadri Banerjee, who in reading drafts of this book graciously donated that scarce and ever elusive commodity of time along with an abundance of insight, gentle critique, and even more important, constructive suggestions for change. Nonetheless, the shortcomings of this volume are decidedly and stubbornly my own.

To my inner circle of beloveds, you know who you are—thank you for still caring as I gave less than I received for far too long; I plan to make it up to you soon. Last but never least, to my children, Jesse and Kaira, who are indelibly a part of everything I am and strive for, and to Paul Roorda, who continues to enthrall and inspire after so many years, my gratitude and love, more than words can ever say.

This book is dedicated to the memory of N. Gerald Barrier, a sturdy beacon in Sikh studies who seemed so easily to embody, truly beyond measure, that rare combination of scholarly excellence, humility, and kindness. He is greatly missed.

WATERLOO, ONTARIO

Chronology

1469–1539   Guru Nanak
1539–1552   Guru Angad (b. 1504)
1552–1574   Guru Amar Das (b. 1479)
1574–1581   Guru Ram Das (b. 1534)
1581–1606   Guru Arjan (b. 1563)
1606–1644   Guru Hargobind (b. 1595)
1644–1661   Guru Har Rai (b. 1630)
1661–1664   Guru Har Krishan (b. 1656)
1664–1675   Guru Tegh Bahadur (b. 1621)
1675–1708   Guru Gobind Singh (b. 1666)
- 1699 Creation of the Khalsa order
- Establishment of Sikh scripture as the Guru Granth Sahib

1780–1839   Life of Maharajah Ranjit Singh
1849   Annexation of Punjab by British
1865   First printed edition of the Guru Granth Sahib
1873   Singh Sabha established
1919   Jallianwala Bagh Massacre
1920   Shiromani Gurdwara Parbandhak Committee established
1925   Punjab Gurdwara Act
1947   Indian independence, partition, and creation of Pakistan
1966   Punjabi Suba movement
1980s   Agitation for Khalistan
- 1984 Operation Bluestar

1999   Third centennial of the Khalsa order
2004   Dr. Manmohan Singh becomes first Sikh prime minister of India

Introduction

The idea for this book came while I was listening to a concert in Delhi highlighting some of the ancient musical instruments of India, in particular the *rabaab,* a stringed instrument of exquisite sound and beauty. Its haunting notes transported me back five hundred years to the very beginnings of the religion known as Sikhism, when a mystic known as Nanak composed hymns expounding the glory of the Divine. Accompanied by the Muslim minstrel Mardana playing the *rabaab,* Nanak—known later to his followers as Guru Nanak— wandered the vast countryside of what was then the northern reaches of India, areas located today in the modern nation-states of Pakistan and India, singing and playing hymns to the Divine. Nanak chose the universal language of music to give expression to the inexpressible nature of the Ultimate and humanity's relationship to it.

It is said the Sikh tradition began with music. When Nanak, at the age of thirty, entered the river Bein for his morning bath, he miraculously disappeared. The story relates that, during the three days he was absent from the world, Guru Nanak was ushered into the presence of the Divine and offered a cup of the nectar of immortality. Upon drinking the nectar he suddenly understood the core of spirituality. After returning from his heavenly sojourn, his first words were, "There is no Hindu, there is no Muslim." It is as though he understood that these identifiers that so often act as barriers between people are blinders to what is truly important, to the essence of true religion. Loving the Divine, attuning oneself to the Divine, according to the guru, goes beyond sectarian divisions, beyond the rational confines of the mind. True devotion to the Divine is a matter of the heart. The power of that experience in God's presence was utterly beyond the capability of mere words, and so Guru Nanak turned to music to give *voice* and *meaning* to his vision. Sikhs honor that vision by making *kirtan,* the communal singing of hymns, the pivotal aspect of Sikh congregational life.

As a scholar of the Sikh tradition and an educator, I have often been frustrated by the disparity between how Sikhism and Sikhs are presented in textbooks and the lived realities of Sikhs that I have observed in numerous travels in India and through extensive interaction with Sikhs. Textbook representations are often incomplete, portraying an overly homogeneous image of what it means to be Sikh. Or, the differences between Sikhs and Hindus and Muslims, and in some cases, the animosity between them, are exaggerated. Yet when visiting India the ease with which members of these communities interact, worship, or celebrate together can be striking. Certainly this has been my own experience. While tensions, occasionally violent, between the different religious groups of India exist and will continue to exist, they are often actually political in nature. The relative lack of tension tends to get lost in an overemphasis on these incidents of animosity, leaving readers with the false impression of permanent chasms separating the religious communities in India.

The first time my family and I went to Amritsar to visit Harimandir Sahib, also known as the Golden Temple, a group of university students offered to accompany us to this most sacred shrine. One young man was especially enthusiastic about our first visit and entertained us with stories about the history, significance, and architectural styles of Harimandir Sahib. We wandered along the promenade surrounding the pool, marveling at the beauty of the temple's white marble gleaming in the sun and its shining golden dome. We made our way across the causeway over the pool to the Guru Granth Sahib, the sacred scripture at the heart of the temple.

The temple interior is stunning, with gorgeous brocade surrounding the holy book; the adoration on the faces of devotees and deep sense of peace there were striking. As we left, I questioned our young guide about his own response to Harimandir Sahib. To my surprise, he was not a Sikh but a Muslim! I commented on his speaking of the shrine as if it were holy to him. He replied, "I love the Harimandir as though it were my own. I worship there, I am welcome there. I bow before the Guru Granth Sahib because it contains the poetry and wisdom of Muslims and Hindus. It is a truly universal scripture." When I expressed my amazement at the diversity of our student guides, the Sikhs in our group put their arms around their companions and insisted that "here we are all brothers." Clearly, an openness toward all regardless of creed or caste that is central to Guru Nanak's message and to this dynamic tradition continues to reverberate across the centuries.

Similarly, visitors to the Durga temple in Patiala, Punjab, may witness there Sikhs making offerings to the goddess—even though Sikhs reject the worship of images! Sikhism is monotheistic, and Sikhs insist that their reverence of scripture should not be perceived as worship but instead as an intense act of respect to their guru. In fact, one can observe Sikhs, Hindus, and Muslims intermingling at places of worship, especially during festivals and the many religious celebrations throughout the year. The horrors of the partitioning of India and Pakistan and its attendant slaughter of Hindus, Muslims, and Sikhs are especially sad in light of this more usual ease. Operation Bluestar in 1984, when Prime Minister Indira Gandhi sent troops into Harimandir Sahib to flush out militant Sikhs who had taken refuge there, represents another example of Hindu and Sikh antagonism with tragic results. Many Sikhs vowed never to forget or forgive the attack. Despite this intermittent communal violence, Hindus, Sikhs, and Muslims continue to live peaceably in Punjab and other parts of India.

If discerning the boundaries between religions in India is at times difficult, internal differentiations can also be complicated. I had the privilege of accompanying a Sikh friend to a famous holy center in Punjab called Bhaini Sahib, the nucleus of the Namdhari Sikhs. Namdharis rose to prominence as revolutionaries during the time of British rule in India; Bhaini Sahib represents the ideals of Sikhism as interpreted by the Namdharis. Adherents wear white, often hand-spun traditional Punjabi clothing, live communally, and revere their living guru, who is understood as a necessary guide in the modern world. My companion and I were granted an audience with Satguru Jagjit Singh, the aged leader of Namdharis worldwide; his powerful but gentle presence seemed to fill the room.

Though often criticized, and sometimes ostracized, by some mainstream Sikhs because of the Namdhari Sikhs' belief in a living guru and their rejection of the Guru Granth Sahib as the final and ultimate authority for Sikhs, I was also struck by how easily mainstream Sikhs mingle with Namdharis at Bhaini Sahib. Visiting Sikhs also offered obeisance to Satguru Jagjit Singh and joined in the singing resounding throughout the center. Most Sikhs take great pride in their brave Namdhari brothers and sisters who stood up to British rule long before Mohandas Gandhi's Quit India Movement. When I asked my Sikh companion why he came to Bhaini Sahib, he answered that coming to the center "gives me peace." This lesson in the religious diversity of the Sikhs has stayed with me and taught me the importance of avoiding speaking of Sikhism as a homogeneous faith and tradition.

ORGANIZATION OF THE BOOK
When considering the length and content of the chapters in this volume, I was reminded of a conversation I had had with a Sikh friend about what is central to Sikhs in their tradition. He suggested that if I were to ask an average Sikh in the Western world—a restaurant owner in Boston, a factory worker in Birmingham, a bank teller in Rome, or a university student in Canada—about an aspect of Sikh history, I would be amazed at how knowledgeable they would be about their history. It is indeed intriguing how primary Sikh history is to those of Sikh heritage. This is not accidental. The *ardas,* the formal petition or request that concludes virtually every Sikh ritual or religious gathering, recalls various aspects of the Sikh past. Because of the prayer's centrality in devotional and congregational life, Sikhs cannot but remember their own glorious history, especially the martyred heroes who died for the sake of justice and devotion.

This preoccupation with Sikh history is also mirrored in Sikh studies. Although some recent scholarship has argued that Sikh history has become *too* much the focus of academic study, to the detriment of other aspects of the discipline, the reality is that the study of Sikh history continues to offer a fruitful arena of research. It is highly unlikely that this focus will wane in the near future. For these reasons, the history of the Sikhs forms the largest portion of this volume.

Nonetheless, I begin with an overview of the main textual sources of the Sikh tradition. As noted, the Guru Granth Sahib is, at least for mainstream Sikhs, at the center of all religious devotion, and it is there that the discussion of Sikhism begins. After the introduction to this and other important texts, and the importance of music in its structure and organization, chapter 2 turns to the history of Sikhism.

It begins with the marvelous stories associated with the founder of Sikhism in the fifteenth century and concludes with the momentous election of India's first Sikh prime minister in 2004. Chapter 3 describes the teachings, rituals, practices, and festivals of the Sikh religion. Issues of Sikh identity are also explored, an important feature of Sikhism both historically and in the present day. Chapter 4 takes up various aspects of Sikh society, focusing on the Sikh homeland of Punjab in northern India. For Sikhs, the family unit is the backbone of society; the family system and social patterns, including caste within Sikhism, thus also take a significant share of this chapter. Chapter 5 is devoted to the Sikh diaspora, an important subject given the increasing population of this community worldwide. Chapter 6 considers the diversity of Sikh identity, specifically distinct groups included under the umbrella of "Sikhism." The volume concludes with a brief look at Sikhs and Sikhism in the twenty-first century and beyond.

The term "Sikh" means "learner," and in my exploration of Sikhism, I see myself as a learner, a student of a tradition that I have come to love, one that in my own spiritual journey has urged me to the heights and depths of self-discovery. It has stirred yearnings toward what Sikhs call the *anhad shabad* (unstruck melody), that mysterious music pervasive in the universe generated by the Divine and heard only by the soul. I invite you to join me in this exploration of a little-known though rich tradition that has much to offer an often troubled world.

CHAPTER 1

The Sources of the Sikh Tradition

Guru Granth Sahib. Courtesy of Harjant Gill.

Scholars of Sikhism generally turn to the Sikh scripture known as the Adi Granth (Original Volume). Sikhs refer to this scripture as the Guru Granth Sahib or Sri Guru Granth Sahib. They view their scripture as much more than a mere book; it is the abode of the gurus, the repository of the words of Akal Purakh (Eternal Being) transcribed by their Sikh masters. It is the Divine in material form. As such, the text is understood as the eternal and living guru of the Sikhs.

The term "guru" in Indian religious contexts refers to an enlightened master, one who passes spiritual knowledge to a devotee. For Sikhs, the term "guru" has several meanings, as reflected in Sikh scripture. The ten Sikh gurus are seen as enlightened masters who had received a message of liberation from Akal Purakh. Therefore,

Akal Purakh may also be referred to as Guru in scripture, with the ten Sikh gurus understood to be mediators of divine wisdom. The content of Sikh scripture is known variously as *bani* (utterance), *gurbani* (utterance of the Guru), and *shabad* (divine word). In essence then, Sikh scripture is revelatory, communicated by the Sikh gurus and other enlightened individuals as timeless correspondence between Akal Purakh and humanity.

When Guru Gobind Singh, the tenth and last master, ended the living guru lineage, adoration and reverence were to focus instead on the eternal message of the gurus. Thus, Sikh scripture has been known as the Sri Guru Granth Sahib, or simply the Guru Granth Sahib. The term *sri* and the honorific masculine *sahib* are used in the Indian context when referring to a male who is in a respectful position. The word *sahib* is also added to historically and ritually important shrines of the Sikh tradition, including Harimandir Sahib in Amritsar.

The Guru Granth Sahib contains a number of vernacular languages current at the time of its writing, including Braj and Sant Bhasa, which are similar to modern Punjabi and Hindi. It was written in the Gurmukhi script, which was widely used among the merchant classes at the time of the gurus. It is important to note that the Guru Granth Sahib was not written in Sanskrit, the holy language of the priestly classes; this decision of the Sikh gurus arose from their desire that their verses be accessible to all classes, perhaps especially to those not knowledgeable in Sanskrit, the language of the elite.

The earliest anthology of Sikh hymns, known as the Goindval volume, was first collected by the third guru of the Sikhs, Guru Amar Das. A more substantial version was compiled by the fifth guru, Guru Arjan, who also included his own compositions and selected hymns by a number of other poet-saints from both Hindu and Muslim traditions. They include hymns by the poet-saints Kabir, Namdev, and Ravidas, among others. All the hymns chosen for the Guru Granth Sahib reflected the spiritual worldview of the gurus. Many other poet-saints' compositions not clearly aligned with Sikh thought, particularly in terms of the absolute oneness of the Divine, were thus excluded. This collection by Guru Arjan, completed in 1604, came to be known as the Kartarpur volume.

The development of Sikh scripture was brought to completion upon Guru Gobind Singh's addition of hymns composed by his father, Guru Tegh Bahadur; Guru Gobind Singh did not include his own masterfully written compositions. Following Guru Gobind Singh's death, the scripture of the Sikhs began to be identified as the Guru of the Sikhs, the sacred volume that is the Guru. Mainstream Sikhs still consider it the embodiment of the Eternal Guru that signaled the end of the living guru lineage. Whereas the title Guru Granth Sahib is confessional in character, Adi Granth is an equally correct, though more neutral, name for the Sikh scripture; both titles are used in this book.

Sikhs believe that the light that shone brightly in the body of the first guru, Nanak, was also present in the bodies of all subsequent gurus. This is given practical expression in the labeling of the compositions of each guru according to his place in the guru succession, rather than by his name. The hymns of Guru Nanak are thus labeled Mahala 1, and Guru Angad's compositions are signed Mahala 2. The actual meaning of the term *mahala* is obscure but was likely borrowed from Islam, where it refers to the notion of principality or abode. The gurus' writings are thus "the place where the Divine resides."

The Adi Granth, totaling 1,430 pages, contains the writings of six of the ten Sikh gurus and of various other poet-saints. It is organized chronologically, beginning with the hymns of the Sikh gurus and ending with the compositions of the other poet-saints. The collection is unique among the world's scriptures in being made up mainly of hymns to be sung rather than text to be read or recited. It is not a series of stories, parables, or philosophical statements; nor is it a set of ethical precepts, arguments, or a historical account. It is a work in which music is integral. The hymns praise Nirgun (Formless One), among other names, and by their singing the devotee is believed to be brought into a mystical union with Nirgun. The exceptions are the Mul Mantra and Japji Sahib, which are instead recited. The Mul Mantra is the statement of creed at the beginning of the Guru Granth Sahib; it functions as a liturgical prologue outlining the fundamental doctrine of the oneness, greatness, and omnipotence of God. The Japji Sahib, an exquisite hymn of praise to the Divine, immediately follows the Mul Mantra. These opening stanzas are recited by Sikhs daily upon waking from sleep.

The primacy of music to Sikh scripture and devotional life is beautifully illustrated in the carefully constructed framework of the Guru Granth Sahib. It has thirty-one divisions, or musical measures, known as *rags*. The term *rag* stems from the Sanskrit root *ranj*, which means to "color with emotion." Reflecting this basic meaning, *rags* are Indian musical or melodic formulae that were composed and arranged to create a particular mood or atmosphere. However, they are also imbued with spiritual significance. According to ancient theories of Indian music, the physical vibrations of musical sound are intimately connected with worlds beyond the physical realm. *Rags* are believed to exist eternally and thus are discovered, rather than created, by inspired musicians. Correct musical pitch and tone and the numbers of vibrations in *rags* are interconnected and lead ultimately to the well-being of the universe. They are also reflective of the natural order; some are to be sung in the morning, others in the evening. Some *rags* evoke yearning relating to the harvest season; others give a sense of delight and anticipation for the coming year. Particular melodic modes produce feelings of joy and are sung during weddings or to celebrate birth, while others lead to a sense of deep contentment. Still others suggest grieving. In performance, the exact number of vibrations must be maintained in order to attain the mood ascribed to a specific *rag*. In the Sikh context, *rags* express the gurus' understanding of the natural changes in life, both positive and negative, and of the need to live through such times in balance.

The genius of the Sikh gurus in the writing and collecting of these hymns is that they emphasized Sikh philosophical reflections on the nature of the Formless One while also offering an invitation to engage through music in the spiritual quest collectively or in solitude. By means of this musical reflection on the nature of Akal Purakh, the gurus taught their devotees to take an active part in their own spiritual transformations. Consequently, these devotional expressions in song are understood as a means of spiritual transformation. I. J. Singh, a modern-day Sikh writer, beautifully describes this centrality of music:

> The fact that the hymns of the Guru Granth are principally composed in the classical mode of music tells me that the Gurus truly explored and celebrated the Ultimate Reality through the magic

and mystery of music. The beauty of this is what they wished to communicate and teach . . . Ultimately, the goal of kirtan lies beyond even that . . . Its goal is to train the inner ear—the heart and soul—that responds and vibrates to the celestial music within, music that springs without a chord being struck and requires no musical instrument except that of a willing and open heart. This is what the Gurus intended. (I. J. Singh 2003, 65–71)

Clearly, the gurus aligned themselves with ancient Indian theories of sound and its transformative nature. The power of sound itself together with the meaning of the hymns was believed to purify the mind and thus lead to lives of devotion and spirituality. Above all, the Guru Granth Sahib is a collection of hymns praising Akal Purakh and a message of spiritual liberation for all. Through loving devotion to God and the practical meditative techniques taught by the gurus, liberation was open to anyone, regardless of caste, creed, gender, or race. On the other hand, as a magnificent ode to the Ultimate, it contains little about the historical development of Sikhism.

Issues of interpretation and translation of this sacred scripture have increasingly come to the fore with the transmission of Sikhism to far-flung lands. Many second- and third-generation Sikhs living outside Punjab are not fluent in Punjabi and cannot read the Gurmukhi script of the Guru Granth Sahib. The script is often unreadable even by fluent speakers of Punjabi. Therefore, though the gurus made a concerted effort to compose their hymns in the vernacular of Punjab so their messages would be accessible to all, over time the script and language of the scripture have grown remote and, at the same time, acquired a somewhat sacred status. For this reason translations are generally not acceptable in Sikh *gurdwaras* (literally, "gateway to the guru," a Sikh place of worship) around the world. In some *gurdwaras* outside Punjab, however, efforts are being made to make the text accessible through technological innovations such as projections that include the Gurmukhi, Punjabi in Roman script, and English. Obviously, this issue will remain important for future generations of Sikhs to address.

Another aspect of the Guru Granth Sahib has to do with gendered language. Although often translated or interpreted into masculine-dominated language and imagery, it is important to note that the gurus used both male and female imagery to describe the characteristics of the Divine. The mystical union between God and the devotee is often rendered according to the relationship between female and male. The gurus understood that God cannot be bound by categories of gender.

Dasam Granth

Another important volume for Sikhs is the Dasam Granth (*dasam* means "tenth"), which contains the writings of the tenth guru, Gobind Singh. Its authorship is controversial, however, since many believe it also includes compositions by other writers from the guru's court. The Dasam Granth is more varied in content than the Guru Granth Sahib, including not only devotional hymns but also ancient legends and tales, characterized as "the wiles of women," popular anecdotes, and a letter known as Zafarnama addressed to the Mogul emperor Aurangzeb, who ruled over much of India during the lifetime of Guru Gobind Singh. Some of this content many Sikhs find questionable.

Whereas much of the Dasam Granth plays a lesser role in the devotional lives of Sikhs, certain hymns are recited daily, especially those attributed to Guru Gobind Singh. There are groups within the wider Sikh community by which the Dasam Granth is held in high esteem and given nearly the same respect as the Guru Granth Sahib, but for the vast majority of Sikhs, the Dasam Granth is not conferred the same status as the Guru Granth Sahib.

Janamsakhis

Another category of important texts, the *janamsakhis,* or *sakhis,* are collections of hagiographic anecdotes focusing on the life of the first guru, Nanak. The earliest collections were later expanded to include stories related to the later gurus and are thus grouped in the *janamsakhi* genre. Though the *janamsakhis* and subsequent narratives cannot be understood as having a sacred status, they hold an important place in Sikhism. Since the Adi Granth offers little historical information about their gurus, Sikhs turn to these stories to learn about the lives of the gurus, their families, the miraculous occurrences surrounding them, and the difficulties caused by the gurus' political and religious opponents. Nonetheless, they are questionable as reliable historical sources since they were written well after the time of the gurus. Moreover, the *janamsakhis* are not consistent with one another. However, they do offer important insights into the development of the early Sikh tradition. They are best taken as testimonies of faith, offering glimpses as to how the early Sikh followers viewed and understood the lives and missions of their gurus. Working within narratives that are consistent with one another in the *janamsakhis,* scholars can attempt to piece together a more accurate account of the historical development of Sikhism.

Sikh Reht Maryada

Another primary text is the Sikh Reht Maryada. It is the Sikh code of conduct and, in its present form, stems from the mid-twentieth century. It has two sections, the first focusing on personal discipline and the second on wider community concerns. It defines Sikh religious identity, including correct Sikh behavior and things to avoid, proper ways of conducting rituals of birth, marriage, and death, as well as a number of other personal and community disciplines.

According to tradition, the nucleus of the code of conduct can be traced to the time of Guru Gobind Singh. With time and its changes, additions were made to the original precepts. However, there were numerous versions of this code throughout the eighteenth and nineteenth centuries. As a result, Sikh reformers of the latter nineteenth century began the painstaking task of drafting a version acceptable to the needs and expectations of their contemporaries while remaining true to the central message of Sikhism. Not until 1932 was an initial draft completed, and after many revisions, the version considered authoritative by Sikhs today, the Sikh Reht Maryada, was published in 1950. Despite the diversity in Sikhism, the 1950 code of conduct clearly reflects the ideals of the Khalsa Sikh form and identity instituted by the tenth guru, Gobind Singh.

CHAPTER 2

Sikh History

The writing of history is a difficult, complex activity. Different assessments of what is historically accurate tend to offer varied accounts of what actually took place in a particular community or religion. For historians, the factuality of an incident or event is obviously central. Attempts are made to analyze as many perspectives and counterperspectives as possible to ensure an incident actually occurred. Scholars of history are acutely aware that at times accounts depicting a certain incident have a great deal to do with subsequent interpretations of the event. Thus, the dating and authentication of texts is crucial in historical research.

Writing History

For a richer understanding of religious history, scholars often turn to the narratives of a religious community, for storytelling is an essential activity in the life of every society. While well-loved narratives may form an important part of piecing together a history of a religious community, there may be little historical evidence to support them. Historians may then question how these narratives serve to *make sense* of a particular event or development in a community. This is especially important when investigating the history of a community that has traditionally placed little value on the textual documentation of events, or when examining the histories of illiterate communities that have relied on oral traditions. If the stories in such communities move from oral transmission to a written form, scholars are increasingly aware of the need to question who is doing the writing and why this change in transmission is taking place. Most members of such communities have had little access to the written word; the written transmission of a particular account has traditionally been left to a small minority, namely, the elite or the learned of any particular society. Moreover, these writings have tended to ignore or even dismiss the realities of those outside this small group. Consequently, often what *has* been written has served the interests of that minority. At the very least, then, such textual transmissions offer little insight into the lives and values of the common people. Traditional historical accounts have tended to focus on the businesses of war, politics, and intrigue. These aspects of history were, quite obviously, considered important to those in power, yet these accounts say little about the everyday realities of the majority of the population in a given society.

Much of this holds true when attempting to piece together the history of a religious tradition. Scholars have traditionally looked to the written word, especially sacred texts, to understand the main tenets of a particular tradition. By studying the sacred texts of a tradition, one gains insight into its view of the Divine, the role of religious intermediaries, notions of good and evil, and the relationship between humanity and the Divine. Secondary written sources, for example commentaries, add to such knowledge. Narratives and moral tales also offer insights into what is considered ideal or approved behavior in a particular religious community.

Although the focus on texts is clearly important for understanding any religious community, it is equally worthwhile to consider that the worldview of the other members of a tradition are usually absent from these texts. These histories are mostly silent about women's realities, for example. In recent years, feminist scholars have begun the painstaking work of collecting fragments of history providing insights into women's roles in a particular community. Women have traditionally been perceived as not having taken an active role in war, politics, or economics, at least not on a scale deemed mentionable. It is often in connection with regulating women's behavior that they gain entry into histories. Scholars may question what forces caused a particular concern or regulation to arise. This course of analysis leads to another complicating issue; namely, while codes

of conduct offer information about correct behavior, beliefs, or rituals in a religious tradition, such proscriptions may say more about
the values and expectations of religious specialists in a tradition
than about the realities of ordinary people. Historians are thus re-
alizing that it is important to study history from the perspective of
those forgotten in textual sources, one that also looks for evidence of
the everyday lives of ordinary people. Approaches vary but can include examining alternative practices of women and other subject
classes of people, archaeological evidence, art forms (including tex-
tiles, traditionally the work of women), songs, and oral narratives,
among others. Obviously, the writing of history—of a people, society,
or religious community—is complex and requires curiosity, creativ-
ity, sensitivity, and rigorous training in historical methodologies and
frameworks for approaching history.

This is no less true regarding Sikh history. Though Sikhism is a
relatively young tradition, it offers a fascinating picture of the inter-
play between traditions that were first oral and later textual. Scholars
often disagree as to the extent to which the earliest written evidence
can be considered an authentic version of actual events, relative to
later texts, which tend to offer more detailed explanations of the same
events. Questions also arise as to whether certain tellings have been
embellished, or whether a text is simply reflective of the needs of a
later society attempting to make sense of a specific situation or event.
It is also possible that the writers of later texts were able to include
oral traditions that were for some reason not taken into account in
the earlier texts. This possibility of course complicates attempts to
determine accuracy. In such cases, historians compare mentions of
an incident in as many sources as possible.

These questions become important when looking at the hagiographic literature known as the *janamsakhis* (literally, "birth stories"). These anecdotes about the life of Guru Nanak existed in oral
form from the time of the guru and were put in written form well after the his death. Later texts used similar formats to narrate the lives
of subsequent gurus. While not strictly *janamsakhis*, they are included in the *janamsakhi* genre. Although these narratives form the
backdrop of much of what is known of the developing Sikh tradition,

there is much that is historically questionable in these texts. First, they were generally written well after the time of the events and the individuals they portray. Second, there are discrepancies between the various versions of *janamsakhi* narratives. Third, when portrayals in the narratives of incidents are compared with accounts in records outside the Sikh tradition, official government records, for instance, the inconsistencies are often significant. This is not unusual or necessarily problematic, but it does point to questions of who is representing history and for what reasons. Another interesting feature of the *janamsakhis* is that they often borrowed from earlier narrative traditions, such as the Jataka tales depicting the life of Gautama Buddha, the founder of Buddhism. One such story tells of the great king of the serpents, Mucalinda, protecting the meditating Gautama Buddha under the bodhi tree from the elements with his giant hood. In the Sikh context, Guru Nanak, having fallen asleep under a tree, is protected from the sun's glare by a giant cobra. The question then arises whether the writers of his story attempted to place Guru Nanak in a lineage of spiritual masters by depicting him in a similar situation.

In looking at Sikh history, scholars often attempt to isolate the strictly empirical, in other words, what can be proven, from what is clearly anecdotal and serves to explain the community's ideals. For many Sikhs, these narratives are authentic accounts and attempting such distinctions verges on sacrilege and, at the very least, a dishonoring of important aspects of Sikh history. This is especially true for accounts of miraculous events resulting from their gurus' piety and divine powers. Assessing the historical accuracy of such incidents is obviously problematic for scholars relying on conventional methods of historical analysis and criticism. In an attempt to offer readers a glimpse into the richness of Sikh history and its early development, based largely on *janamsakhi* sources, I present in some cases differing versions of a particular incident. Locutions such as "Sikh tradition" or "popular accounts" serve to identify anecdotes or descriptions that may be at variance with historians' conclusions but nonetheless offer important insights into deeply held convictions in the community in terms of its identity, beliefs, and history.

Guru Nanak

Fifteenth-century Punjab witnessed the origin of what we refer to today as Sikhism with the birth of Nanak in 1469 in the village of Talwandi, now known as Nankana Sahib and located southwest of Lahore in Pakistan. As the first guru of the Sikhs, Nanak has received more attention than any of his nine successors. This is due not only to his importance as founder of Sikhism but also to the many wondrous stories depicting his great charisma, piety, and goodness in the *janamsakhis*.

Nanak was born a Hindu in the Khatri caste, a mercantile Punjabi lineage. Nanak's father, Kalu Bedi, was a bookkeeper who worked as a revenue official. His mother's name was Tripta, and he had an elder sister, Nanaki. The *janamsakhis* tell of his being greeted at birth by heavenly hosts, a sure sign of his destined greatness; his midwife was amazed when she heard the infant laughing as though he were a grown man. The venerable scholar to whom Kalu Bedi rushed following his son's birth proclaimed that the stars had aligned to ensure a bright future for the boy. Upon seeing the child, the scholar foretold of Nanak's name becoming known both in the heavens and on earth. The wonders surrounding Nanak continued. At seven months, Nanak would sit in a yoga position with his legs drawn underneath him, despite his parents' attempts to relieve him. As a child, Nanak observed in awe the birds and beasts, the trees, flowers, and the seasons. These experiences later infused Guru Nanak's message and his understanding of Akal Purakh's manifestations in the world.

At the proper time, Kalu Bedi accompanied Nanak to the village school. Within days, Nanak was composing poetry and asking his teacher questions far beyond his years. But the accounting skills Kalu had anticipated his son would learn in order to follow in his father's footsteps evaded Nanak, despite his father's and teacher's best efforts. Yet he was well versed in Persian, Sanskrit, and basic Arabic and eventually did learn the rudiments of what he needed for the mercantile world.

During these years his thirteen-year-old sister, Nanaki, was married to Jairam, an employee of the governor of Sultanpur. The departure of his beloved sister caused Nanak great anguish. When Nanak was eleven years old, another significant event took place, the conferring of the sacred cord worn around the neck and over the shoulder by upper-caste Hindu males, those known as twice born and thus distinguishable from members of the lower castes. According to the *janamsakhi* accounts, however, Nanak spurned the cotton cord, insisting that humanity should not to be divided into high and low. His surprising response caused a great stir in the village, many seeing his action as a disgrace to his family and a revolt against a sacred custom.

Kalu Bedi began to despair of his son's settling into a proper course in life. Often when Nanak was sent to the fields to tend the buffalo, he would spend the time in deep meditation, oblivious of the herd in his charge. Other times he could be found sitting at the feet of wayfaring sadhus, Hindu ascetics, or wandering Sufi dervishes, Muslim mystical teachers, who happened through the village. There are many stories of miraculous events in Nanak's early years. In one, while Nanak was lost in meditation, his buffalo broke into a neighbor's field and began grazing on the newly sown crop. The furious owner reported the incident to the village chief, who admonished Nanak and ordered that the farmer be compensated. However, when it came to assessing the damage, it was discovered that not a single leaf had been harmed! The amazed farmer proclaimed a miracle had taken place. An important shrine at Nankana Sahib commemorates the place where this event is said to have occurred.

Another story tells of Nanak sleeping in a field while a giant cobra spread its hood to shield the young Nanak from the burning sun. Witnesses declared the youth was no ordinary mortal and hurried back to the village to extol Nanak's virtues to his father. But Kalu Bedi's worries about his son only increased as Nanak became more and more immersed in otherworldly thoughts. Nanak explained to his father that his own heart was a temple and to it he was drawn as he went about his daily life. When Nanak stopped eating and drinking for extended periods of time, his family called in physicians and holy men, but they could not find what was ailing the young man. Accounts tell of Nanak finally rousing himself and telling those around him that his ailment was not physical but came instead from his desire for an enlightened mind and spirit.

Nanak, the first guru, and Mardana. Poster, 2003.
Courtesy of Kapany Collection of Sikh Art.

Soon after, Nanak traveled to Sultanpur to stay with Nanaki's new family. Once there, Nanak began managing the granaries with surprising enterprise. The *janamsakhis* describe how Nanak spent his days in Sultanpur. Just before daybreak, he rose and bathed in the nearby river Bein, meditated on the divine name, and spent the rest of the day in transactions with the people of the town. Evenings he prayed and sang hymns to the glory of God. While in Sultanpur Nanak reunited with his boyhood friend, Mardana, a low-caste village bard who recorded family genealogies as a profession. Despite the strict societal regulations proscribing this sort of interaction between high and low castes, Mardana became Nanak's constant companion. An accomplished player of the stringed instrument called the *rabaab*, he accompanied Nanak's mystical hymns of devotion.

Although accounts do not make clear when, Nanak was likely in his early to midteens when he married a girl named Sulakhani. Two boys were born to them, Srichand and Lakhshmidas. The family settled into the comfortable lifestyle of the merchant caste. But one day after his morning bath, Nanak did not return to the village. His clothes were found on the bank of the river Bein, but he was nowhere to be seen. Nets were thrown into the water in search of his corpse, but found nothing. Nanak's family and friends fell into grief and despair. Then, three days later, he reappeared.

In one of Nanak's sacred compositions, he recounts the incident that abruptly changed his life. When he entered the river for his daily ablutions, he found himself ushered into the presence of Akal Purakh, where he was given the mission to spread a message of the glory and grace of God. His first words, according to the *janamsakhis*, were, "There is no Hindu, there is no Muslim." Soon after Nanak was called Guru Nanak, enlightened teacher, in acknowledgment of his miraculous experience and mission. Accounts relate that Guru Nanak did not delay in fulfilling his mission; leaving behind his wife and children, he began the first of four missionary travels accompanied by his faithful friend and minstrel, Mardana.

Making no distinction between Hindus and Muslims, Guru Nanak wore the garb traditionally associated with both groups. For this reason he was at times mistaken for a Sufi and at others, a Hindu sadhu. Paintings of Guru Nanak, from long after his time, often depict him as neither a mendicant nor a householder. In one encounter with a leading scholar in Varanasi, the ancient center of Hindu learning, he was questioned about his faith, for Guru Nanak neither carried a devotee's stone or rosary nor wore ashes on his forehead. For his reply, Guru Nanak turned to Mardana and together they offered a hymn extolling the name, virtue, and grace of God.

Guru Nanak traveled for two decades, visiting shrines and pilgrimage sites of different religious affiliations. His compositions reveal an extensive knowledge of the beliefs and practices that he encountered in his journeys. He was conversant in the ways of Sufi and Sunni Islam, Jainism, the various Hindu philosophies and orders, Buddhism, and Zoroastrianism. His writings tell of the many conversations with other wandering mendicants as he traveled in each of the four directions, east to Assam, south to Sri Lanka, north to the mythical Mount Sumeru (believed to correspond to present-day Mount Kailash), and west to the Muslim holy centers of Mecca and Medina. The extent of Guru Nanak's travels is debated by scholars, but Guru Nanak unquestionably traveled widely, sharing his message of universality and Akal Purakh's compassionate love for all.

In the *janamsakhi* accounts of Guru Nanak's travels, a story is told of his arriving in a village near the end of a long day of wandering and immediately heading to the home of a poor, low-caste carpenter. Guru Nanak and Mardana accepted the carpenter's offer of a simple meal and stayed on at the carpenter's home for a time. News of Guru Nanak's appearance in the village and breach of caste custom spread throughout the region. The local Muslim chief invited the newcomers to a great feast in Guru Nanak's honor. The guru insisted, however, that the carpenter's simple fare also be included at the feast. It is said that Guru Nanak took the carpenter's humble food in one hand and the chief's rich offerings in the other. From the carpenter's, drops of milk fell; from the chief's fare, drops of blood spilled. Guru Nanak intended by his act to compare the honest labor of the poor and lowly with the questionable practices of the chief, who had amassed great wealth at the cost of others. The villagers were amazed and Guru Nanak's fame spread far and wide.

Another time, newly arrived in the holy city of Hardwar, in the early morning light Guru Nanak joined other pilgrims in the waters of the Ganges. He observed them immersing themselves and offering their water-filled palms to the rising sun. The guru faced the opposite direction but also with offerings of water. Guru Nanak's lesson was that it didn't matter which direction one faced, Akal Purakh was to be found everywhere; true devotion was in the heart of each and every individual.

Mardana and Guru Nanak were also sorely tested during their travels. In one case, Mardana was bewitched by a beautiful woman who turned out to be a sorcerer; she turned him into a ram. When Guru Nanak went searching for his companion, a host of female conjurers surrounded the guru and attempted to put spells on him too. Though the women danced and sang and called upon their great queen to shower him with treasures, Guru Nanak turned away and began singing a hymn of praise to the Divine. Mardana's spell was broken and, according to the *janamsakhis,* the conjurers threw themselves at the feet of Guru Nanak and vowed to mend their ways.

When Guru Nanak and Mardana arrived in Mecca after a long day of travel, the guru entered the precincts of the holy Ka'aba and lay down to rest. When the time came for evening prayer, a learned man saw the sleeping traveler with his feet facing the Ka'aba, a sacrilege to devout Muslims. He roused Guru Nanak and rebuked him for not showing respect for the holy shrine. Guru Nanak requested that the scholar point the guru's feet in the direction where God did not reside. No matter where he placed Guru Nanak's feet, the Ka'aba followed. The devout scholar hurried away, announcing to all that he had met a true holy man.

Sometime in the early 1520s, Guru Nanak returned to Punjab and established the community eventually known as Kartarpur, located in a beautiful setting near present-day Lahore. As his charisma and message spread, he attracted a community of followers, who were called Sikhs, meaning "learners" or "disciples." His earliest followers were mainly relatives and other members of the Khatri caste. As the community grew, lower-caste individuals, including Jats, the rural majority in the surrounding areas, also joined the guru's community. And though Mogul rulers discouraged Muslims from affiliating with other teachings, Muslims nonetheless constituted a small contingent of the early followers.

Guru Nanak was very much in line with the larger Bhakti movement, a reform effort that began in the sixth century in southern India and gained momentum in the twelfth century in the west-central
regions of India. The movement reached the north roughly in the
sixteenth century. Bhakti emphasized devotion to the Divine, and
the movement was led by men and women poet-saints who wandered
the countryside singing praises to the Ultimate, similar to the guru's missionary travels. Scholars distinguish within the Bhakti movement between poet-saints who extolled God *with* attributes or form,
namely, *saguna bhaktas,* and those extolling God without and beyond all attributes or form, known as *nirguna bhaktas.* Another distinction has been made within the *nirguna bhakti* strain, namely the
Sants, a mainly north Indian movement that included poet-saints
like Kabir, Dadu, and Nanak. The Sants strongly rejected notions of
the Divine incarnate in images and asceticism as the path to liberation. Liberation was to be attained rather through living fully in the
world. Reflecting their belief in the centrality of personal devotion
without the need for intermediaries, these poet-saints were highly
critical of organized and hierarchical forms of religion. They rejected
caste and gender as barriers to liberation and sang of the importance
of inward spirituality as opposed to empty ritualism, pilgrimages,
and religious insignia.

In this rich milieu Guru Nanak furthered his own profound message of liberation. He added a practical dimension to similar spiritual paths advocated by his contemporaries in his insistence on community life, demonstrated by his Kartarpur site. Through a living
community of Sikhs, he ensured that his teachings would continue
and thrive. The ideal espoused by the guru was that of the householder. Akal Purakh was accessible to all at all times, perhaps even
especially within the worldly structures of society that were renounced by other spiritual masters as inhibiting spiritual development. For Guru Nanak, those structures, the family and the larger
social system, were arenas within which Nirgun, the Formless One,
was to be sought. In other words—the Divine was fully present in the
everyday workings of society. Akal Purakh was as accessible to the
farmer in the field as to the trader in the market. Hymns of praise
were to be constantly on the lips and in the hearts of men and women

in all occupations, at all times, in all places. He further insisted on the primacy of the fellowship of believers, known as the *sangat* (congregation), thus showing the way to peaceful coexistence between individuals and between castes. Guru Nanak taught his followers that singing praise to God would lead to liberation and to lives transformed by service, devotion, and love.

The daily life of the Kartarpur community revolved around the presence and charisma of the guru and the practical implications of his message. This was not a haven for social escapists; work was basic to the community's existence. These first Sikhs rose early, bathed in preparation for the day ahead, and undertook their daily work meditating on the divine name. This discipline was known as *nam simran*. Just as it was then, it is the primary meditative discipline of the Sikhs. The technique involved more than the mere repetition of the many names of the Ultimate; the guru taught that those desiring liberation must sincerely focus on the many and varied attributes of Akal Purakh, who, though of countless names, is beyond all names. Internalizing such an understanding of Akal Purakh would in time lead to transformed lives. Those who meditated on the Formless One and became attuned to that essence were known as *gurmukhs* (those focused on God); those not God focused were called *manmukhs* (those driven by ego). For Guru Nanak and the subsequent gurus, the ultimate purpose of human life was to be a *gurmukh*, one living in unity with the divine will. This could be achieved through diligent practice of *nam simran*, resulting in Akal Purakh's active dwelling in the soul.

Besides daily meditation and work, the guru's followers assembled in the house of the guru, then called a *dharmsala*, to sing the praises of the Creator with other members of the congregation. Congregants sang the guru's compositions accompanied by musical instruments, following the guru's early ministry with Mardana. An initiation ritual known as *charan amrit* or *charan pahul* (nectar of the feet) delineated the early community from surrounding groups. The earliest manifestation of the rite consisted of the guru's toe being dipped in water, that water then drunk by the community. Later, it was the initiate's toe that was immersed in water and that water drunk by followers. In a society concerned with ritual purity and pollution, the guru was demonstrating what he considered to be inconsequential distinctions and meaningless notions of purity and impurity.

More than anything else, however, like bees seeking flowers in springtime, the early followers gathered to receive the blessings of their guru. Paramount in Hindu devotion is the notion of seeing and being seen by the Divine. This ideal extends to being seen by and seeing a spiritual master. By his very presence, in being seen by their beloved Guru Nanak, blessings abounded. Their master had inspired them through his message of liberation for all and his life of service to the community. To be in his presence and a member of the community surrounding him was, for his devotees, an answer to their longing.

Guru Nanak was perceived as one sent by Nirgun to redeem a corrupt society. Bhai Gurdas, the beloved scribe of numerous gurus, noted that religion had become authoritarian, ritualistic, and morally indifferent, showing little concern for the inward transformation of humanity. Rigidly defined religious affiliations had led to social discord. Guru Nanak therefore taught that distinctions between Hindus and Muslims were without worth, and he challenged his followers and society at large to move beyond all distinctions of caste, gender, and creed. These were, he insisted, mere human formulations created to divide. Distinctions as to pure and impure, high and low, had no merit or place for the One who was loving, compassionate, and accessible to all, the very One who called all creation into a life of mystical unity.

The *janamsakhis* note that Guru Nanak's elder son, Srichand, was a pious, deeply spiritual man. Yet he had embraced a life of asceticism as opposed to the householder ideal espoused by his father. According to tradition, Guru Nanak's younger son, Lakhshmidas, had never shown a genuine interest in a life devoted to the spiritual quest. Guru Nanak thus realized near the end of his long, fulfilled life that he would have to look beyond his own family to find a successor, a true *gurmukh* who could lead and inspire the community by a life of devotion. Consequently, he turned to a disciple who had become a part of the Kartarpur community a few years earlier named Lehna. Lehna had been an ardent devotee of the goddess Durga. According to some sources he was an officiant in the rituals connected with the worship of Durga. Lehna had been so moved by a meeting with the guru as he was passing Kartarpur on a pilgrimage honoring the great goddess that he immediately renounced his path of devotion and became a disciple of Guru Nanak's. The *janamsakhis* emphasize Lehna's great obedience, piety, and humility in his service to the guru. Because of these characteristics, Guru Nanak broke with the tradition of appointing the eldest son as successor and chose Lehna as the subsequent leader of the Sikhs. To preclude all possible doubts regarding Guru Nanak's choice, the *janamsakhis* recount many demonstrations of Lehna's devotion to the guru far surpassing that of his sons. As noted, while the historical accuracy of these accounts is questionable, they nonetheless show the later needs of a community attempting to make sense of its guru's acts and teachings that at times completely overturned long-established traditions. There is the story of an incident in which a jug had fallen into a filthy ditch; Srichand refused to pollute himself by retrieving it. Lakhshmidas, conscious of his status as the son of a guru, considered the task too menial. Lehna, in contrast, picked up the jug, cleaned it, and presented it to the guru filled with clean water. In Guru Nanak's worldview, nothing in and of itself can be understood as polluted; by simply washing the jug Lehna demonstrated a complete understanding of Guru Nanak's message.

Shortly before his death, Guru Nanak called his followers to him and installed Lehna as their guru. He placed before Lehna five coins and a coconut, the coins symbolizing the five elements, fire, water, earth, air, and ether, and the coconut representative of the created universe. In doing so he put the natural world as well as worldly and societal conventions under the authority of his successor. Guru Nanak then bowed low before Lehna and offered his beloved disciple a volume of his own hymns, thus entrusting Lehna with his message and bestowing on him full authority. In keeping with the universality of his thought, Guru Nanak also gave Lehna a woolen rosary symbolizing, in the Sufi tradition, renunciation and devotion, as recontextualized in the context of the Kartarpur community of householders. Finally, he gave Lehna a new name, Angad, from the word *ang*, meaning "limb," thus expressing that Angad was as close and connected to his beloved teacher as his own limb; henceforth their teachings were to be understood as one.

At his death, Guru Nanak left a developing community in Kartarpur, disciples living in accordance with the ideal of the householder, and the beginnings of Sikh scripture in the form of hymns, many in written form, others committed to memory and passed on within the community. The rite of initiation into the community of the faithful had also been established. He also left his followers the technique of *nam simran,* the meditative practice guiding his followers in their quest to become *gurmukhs.* From Guru Nanak's example, his disciples had learned that through the daily practices of work and meditation, they could find the path to unity with Akal Purakh. Perhaps most important, Guru Nanak established a clear delineation of succession based not on the traditional family lineage but instead on merit related to piety, humility, and obedience.

Descriptions in the narratives of the time just before and after Guru Nanak's death speak of the inroads he had made in the northern Indian social and religious consciousness. Shortly before the guru's death, members of the Muslim community announced a desire to claim his body as that of a revered Sufi master, to be buried according to Muslim tradition. Hindu followers, on the other hand, insisted that Guru Nanak, born a Hindu, should be cremated according to the Hindu rite. According to tradition, this is what happened: As those surrounding him began to argue about which community the guru belonged to, he opened his eyes and told his Hindu and Muslim disciples to bring sweet-smelling flowers in anticipation of his death. If in the morning after he had died, he explained, the flowers to the left of his body were still fresh, he was to be buried according to Muslim custom. If, however, the flowers to the right of his body were still fresh, he was to be cremated in accordance with Hindu tradition. After the guru had taken his last breath, his followers sat in silent grief. When the sheet covering their guru was lifted, his disciples saw that the flowers on both sides of his body were as fresh and sweet as the moment they had been picked. This beautiful narrative, written long after the guru's death, was an attempt to encourage accord among all the varied adherents who held Guru Nanak's message as their own. It also underscored the lesson at the core of his teachings, "There is no Hindu, there is no Muslim." All are equal in the loving embrace of Akal Purakh.

Guru Angad

Guru Angad (1504–1552) was installed as the successor to Guru Nanak when he was in his thirties. He served as guru to the community from 1539 until his death in 1552. Guru Angad too was renowned for his meditation practice and his simple lifestyle. Following the practices of his predecessor, he rose before light, bathed, then meditated until day's break. Next he offered blessings and teachings to his followers, making known the way to spiritual liberation. Evenings were spent in communal singing and sermons addressed to his followers and visitors to the community. His love of children was so great, it is said, he would keep even powerful rulers waiting while he played with the youngest members of the community.

Though there is evidence of communal cooking and eating in the earlier community, during Angad's guruship the tradition of the *langar* (community kitchen) became an important feature of the community, and it remains a vital part of Sikh daily life worldwide. Borrowed from the Sufi tradition, it brought to reality the egalitarian message of the gurus, requiring members of all castes to sit and eat together, irrespective of who had prepared the food. This was an outrage in a society steeped in notions of purity and caste. Guru Angad's communal kitchen was widely known, and scriptural references acknowledge Mata (Mother) Khivi, Guru Angad's wife, as playing an important role in the community kitchen. It is worth noting that Mata Khivi is the only spouse of any of the gurus mentioned in the Adi Granth. Simple food offered at *gurdwaras* worldwide for rich or poor, high or low caste, with the only requirement that all eat together, has become a hallmark of Sikhism.

Following traditional laws of inheritance of the time, the sons of Guru Nanak were awarded ownership of the site of Kartarpur. Srichand challenged Guru Angad's authority and claimed succession to his father's position. Guru Angad rejected his claim and moved his seat of authority to the village Khadur, in the modern district of Amritsar. The early community established by Guru Nanak at Kartarpur and Guru Angad's community were virtually identical. Neither community celebrated specifically Sikh festivals and holy days, nor did their lifestyles and practices differ greatly from those in the surrounding religious milieu. What held the community together was its devotion to the guru. Its primary focus on the Divine as a means of liberation from the cycle of transmigration and the ideal of the householder were maintained by the Sikh leadership and devotees throughout the guru period of the tradition's development.

Guru Amar Das

During the time of the third guru, Amar Das (1479–1574), however, a number of important changes in the community took place. Amar Das became the leader of the Sikhs at an advanced age. While a precise date is not known because of inconsistencies about his birth date, he likely became guru at the age of seventy-two or seventy-three. He guided the community for twenty-two years, living to close to ninety-five years. He too was born into the Khatri caste and came from a family of traders. He was married and had three or four children, two sons, Mohan and Mohari, and at least one daughter, Bhani, and possibly another, Dani.

The sons of Guru Angad, Dasu and Datu, upon their father's death claimed the Khadur center as their inheritance and themselves as his spiritual heirs. Thus, with Guru Amar Das, the Sikh seat of authority moved once again, this time to the village of Goindval. This was a period of consolidation in the Sikh community, for a new generation of Sikhs was being born into the community instead of adopting the teachings of the gurus as a matter of personal choice and conviction. One of the changes brought about under the guruship of Amar Das was the construction of a well to provide water to the Sikhs and surrounding residents. The well became a place of pilgrimage for Sikhs to which they traveled to bathe and receive the blessings of their guru. In addition, two preexisting harvest festivals, Baisakhi (in spring) and Diwali (in the fall) took on added significance as important festival days during which Sikhs traveled to Goindval. Guru Amar Das also wrote hymns describing birth, marriage, and death ceremonies. The community's kitchen was known for its abundance of food, an indication of the growing prosperity of the center and the increasing population of Sikhs. In response to the growing number of congregations, changes in administration and authority were also made by Guru Amar Das. Carefully chosen individuals were given the authority to travel the countryside preaching the gurus' teachings. By the end of the sixteenth century, the community had become more diverse with regard to caste, and although all the Sikh gurus were of Khatri lineage, the community itself had moved beyond its initial Khatri caste base. Guru Amar Das also composed hymns critical of such practices associated with the Khatris as widow immolation *(sati)*. Female infanticide, practiced in northern India and associated especially with the Khatri and Jat castes, also came under the guru's censure.

Perhaps most important, Guru Amar Das began, with the help of a professional scribe, to collect the compositions of his predecessors as well as the hymns of other poet-saints. The resulting compilation is known as the Goindval Pothi (Goindval Volume). Aware of the rival claims of spiritual authority following the deaths of previous gurus, claims based on their compositions of hymns, Guru Amar Das deemed it necessary to ensure that only legitimate hymns were passed from congregation to congregation, compositions true to the core doctrine of liberation through the practice of *nam simran.*

Guru Ram Das

Following the death of Guru Amar Das in 1574, the guruship passed to his son-in-law Jetha Sodhi, the husband of his daughter Bhani. This marked a deviation in the previously established pattern of successors from outside the guru's family. Jetha Sodhi (1534–1581) was renamed Guru Ram Das, and while also contributing significant changes in the community's development, he was the master of the Sikhs for only seven years. As with previous gurus, his leadership was also challenged; the sons of Guru Amar Das refused to acknowledge their brother-in-law as the rightful heir to the guruship. A new center was thus established at Ramdaspur, later called Amritsar. Indicative of the growing resources available to Guru Ram Das, he soon began the excavation of a sacred pool at Ramdaspur. Scriptural references indicate that this pool was not only a place to remove the dust of the body but also a sacred place where pilgrims could cleanse themselves of their sins. Thus, pilgrimage to the pool came to be understood as a devotional activity, alongside receiving the guru's blessings and the benefits of congregational life at Ramdaspur.

The hymns of Guru Ram Das clearly show that offerings to the guru provided merit. With the guru's rising prosperity and importance came a growing affluence of the Sikhs. The town of Ramdaspur began to attract more and more people as it grew around its center, the sacred pool. These included, besides the cultivators of the land, traders, merchants, artisans, and craftspeople.

A new position of leadership known as the *masand* (literally, "throne" or "raised platform"), or deputy, was created by the fourth guru, attesting to a growing and more administratively complex community. These deputies were pious individuals chosen from within the community who acted as spiritual guides for the growing number of congregations, received tithes on behalf of the guru, and preached the gurus' message of liberation through the discipline of *nam simran*. They also had the authority to initiate devotees into the community through a ritual called *charan amrit* (literally, "foot initiation"). The guruship of Ram Das was thus marked by significant growth of the Sikh community and a corresponding need for greater organization and devolution of authority.

Guru Arjan

Upon the death of Guru Ram Das in 1581, his youngest son, Arjan, was named his successor. With Guru Arjan (1563–1606), Sikh guruship began to follow a new pattern of succession whereby all subsequent gurus were from the male lineage of Sodhi Khatris, the caste lineage of Guru Ram Das. In essence the principle of nomination established by Guru Nanak was to be upheld, but it was henceforth to be restricted to within one particular family lineage. This was an important institutional change that allowed all subsequent successors to have a legal claim on the guru's headquarters at Ramdaspur. Although Guru Ram Das' other sons, Prithi Chand and Mahadev, could claim their shares of the property and income from the center, the site of Ramdaspur would remain the physical and spiritual center of the Sikhs. This change nevertheless did little to alleviate the antagonism of his brother Prithi Chand toward Guru Arjan. References in Guru Arjan's compositions as well as testimony from the guru's scribe attest to the enmity in the guru's family line. Prithi Chand not only rejected his brother's legitimacy as the guru of the Sikhs but also, it is said, attempted to assassinate Guru Arjan's son Hargobind. Ultimately, Prithi Chand established himself as a rival guru.

Guru Arjan enlarged the sacred pool built by his predecessor and added paving and walls. It came to be known as Amritsar (pool of *amrit* [nectar]). He also ordered the construction of a *gurdwara* at its center, which became a place for the Sikhs to worship, receive their guru's blessings, and sing the praises of Nirgun. He thus provided his followers with an important sacred shrine and center for devotional activities. The town of Ramdaspur continued to grow, with its administration in the hands of Guru Arjan. The Sikhs had thus become well established in central Punjab. While the country at large was ruled by the Moguls, Ramdaspur was an autonomous entity within Emperor Akbar's empire. Other towns were also established by the guru as the Sikh population expanded. Guru Arjan's hymns testify to the growing influence of the gurus' message among all four castes, including a small number of devotees from the outcaste group. Muslim members of the congregation are also mentioned. Once yearly, the deputies traveled the region to collect offerings for the guru and his work and gathered selected Sikhs throughout Punjab to meet with the guru. The role of the guru was becoming more complex; Guru Arjan was seen not only as the spiritual master of his devotees but also as their king. Moreover, it was believed that in receiving Guru Arjan's blessings, all sins were removed; following his teachings on the discipline of *nam simran* would lead to true liberation. Still, while taking on the features of a political entity, the community was above all a spiritual collective. Devotional singing continued as the primary collective spiritual activity of the Sikhs.

Given the increase in guruship rivalry, the importance of authentic hymns authorized by the legitimate guru lineage took on added importance, for the gurus' contenders were also composing hymns. Identifying true *gurbani* (utterances of the guru) as opposed to the sham hymns of his rivals became paramount. Working closely with the venerated scribe Bhai Gurdas and based on the earlier Goindval Pothi, Guru Arjan enlarged the collection with the compositions of his predecessor and hymns of other poet-saints with a clear affinity to the message of the Sikh gurus. To this collection he added his own substantial writings, forming a volume known as the Kartarpur Bir

(Kartarpur Volume). A change was also slowly taking place with regard to the Sikh understanding of the nature of a guru. The gurus' compositions were by now viewed as an alternative to the sacred scripture of the Hindus, the Vedas, and that of the Muslims, the Quran. Seeing the gurus' utterances as divine revelation, a parallel prominence was accorded the guru himself. For although the gurus shunned all intimations of divinity, their message was so closely aligned to the will of Akal Purakh that, to their followers, they were the earthly representatives of Akal Purakh.

The untimely death of Guru Arjan in 1606 proved to be a turning point for the Sikh community. Guru Arjan was under the authority of Emperor Jahangir (1569–1627), who had come to power after the death of Emperor Akbar in 1605. Emperor Akbar had offered gifts to the gurus as well as protection and support to the community. Emperor Jahangir, however, grew suspicious of the rising influence of Guru Arjan among the populace of the region. But more important, Jahangir was angered by what he considered to be Guru Arjan's interference in the affairs of the state when it appeared that the guru had aligned himself with a rival as successor to the throne. Consequently, Guru Arjan was ordered by Emperor Jahangir to be executed. Sikh and Mogul accounts are not in accord as to the nature of Guru Arjan's execution, but Sikhs firmly believe that their guru was burned alive by his captors; official Mogul sources relate the incident as a formal execution as a result of political interference. What is clear is that the revered Sikh institution of martyrdom, though a much later ideal, stems from Guru Arjan's death at the hands of his Mogul captors.

Guru Hargobind

According to tradition, Guru Arjan advised his son and successor, Guru Hargobind (1595–1644), to take the leadership of the Sikhs in a new direction. He was to be fully armed, represented by two swords at the young guru's hips. One sword represented *miri* (the power associated with the political realm), the second, *piri* (spiritual power, a term that was associated with *pir*, referring to a superior spiritual leader). The woolen rosary worn by previous gurus was now replaced by a sword belt. Besides being recognized as a spiritual authority, Guru Hargobind also developed a reputation as an avid hunter.

Although it is uncertain whether the terms *miri* and *piri* were introduced into Sikh parlance at this time, there was a change in the role of guru. Guru Hargobind was believed to possess both worldly and spiritual authority. Trusted devotees were trained in martial activities; the guru also had an infantry. In place of their usual offerings of money, devotees were now to bring to the guru horses and arms as tithes. Sikh territories were demarcated from surrounding territories by thorny trees along their boundaries. Guru Hargobind also built a physical seat of temporal power directly across from the central shrine of the Sikhs, Harimandir Sahib. The building was known as the Akal Takht (Immortal Throne), and it was where Guru Hargobind held court. For the defense of Ramdaspur, the guru constructed a fort, and he also expanded Sikh territory into the Shivalik Hills in the Himalayan region, entrusting this new Sikh center to his eldest son, Gurditta.

The reasons for the substantial changes that took place in the Sikh community and its leadership at this time are unclear. The guru's young age was likely a significant factor. Guru Hargobind became guru at the age of eleven and had to rely heavily on trusted leaders in the community for advice. The death of Guru Arjan clearly also played a part in these developments, but social forces were also at work. The constituency of the Sikh community was changing. Members of the Jat caste had by this time become the majority, surpassing the Khatri caste that had heretofore been dominant. Whereas the Khatris occupied administrative and mercantile positions in the region, the Jats were the majority peasant group, closely tied to the land. For the Jats, land was to be defended at all costs. They were also known for their defiance of authority, and it is likely that they brought their combativeness into the growing community. Historians surmise all these factors combined to bring about significant administrative changes among the Sikhs in the early seventeenth century. These developments would become even more pronounced during the time of the tenth master, Guru Gobind Singh.

The activities of the sixth guru, however, soon caught the attention of Emperor Jahangir. Guru Hargobind was detained, as a result, Mogul sources assert, of a fine left unpaid by Guru Arjan. But the guru apparently won the favor of Emperor Jahangir while imprisoned and was released. For the rest of Jahangir's reign, Guru Hargobind and his community were left in peace. This changed dramatically, however, with the death of Emperor Jahangir and the ascension of Emperor Shah Jahan (1592–1666); tensions between the Sikh leadership and the Mogul authorities again sharpened. A number of skirmishes between Guru Hargobind's forces and those of the emperor ensued, the first involving the capture by the guru's retinue of one of Emperor Shah Jahan's hawks, and the second the seizure of two of Guru Hargobind's horses by the emperor's troops. These were subsequently recaptured by a loyal servant of the guru. These and other confrontations eventually led Guru Hargobind to move his center from Ramdaspur to the Shivalik Hills, where Guru Hargobind led his Sikhs until his death in 1644.

Thus, though in its earliest days the discipline of *nam simran* was the community's core identity, both external and internal forces were creating important changes. These forces included the political milieu but also intra-Sikh tensions. The earlier guruship rivalry came to a head with Guru Hargobind's move to the Shivalik Hills. Ramdaspur was taken over by Miharban, the son of Prithi Chand, who, it will be recalled, previously challenged his brother Guru Arjan's legitimacy. Miharban asserted his legitimacy by continuing the practice of earlier gurus, from Guru Angad to Guru Arjan, who had signed their compositions in the name of Guru Nanak. When Harji, Miharban's son, assumed the leadership upon his father's death, he was known as the eighth Nanak.

Guru succession became increasingly complex. Guru Hargobind had three wives and a total of six children, five of whom were sons. For various reasons, the guru had originally chosen his eldest son, Gurditta, who, though leaning toward the ascetic path, had been given considerable authority at the Shivalik Hills center. However, Gurditta died before his father. Gurditta's son Dhir Mal was another obvious choice, but he was viewed as unreceptive, if not hostile, to the community's needs. Dhir Mal had established his own center in Kartarpur, where he had been given revenue-free land by Emperor Shah Jahan.

Guru Har Rai and Guru Har Krishan

Guru Hargobind turned, rather, to his grandson, Har Rai (1630–1661), the younger brother of Dhir Mal and son of Gurditta, as his successor, at the young age of fourteen. According to the narratives describing this succession, Guru Har Rai had a heart open to all living things; as a child, hurrying to see his beloved grandfather Guru Hargobind, he caught his robe on a bush and broke several of its flowers. Tears filled his eyes when he realized painfully he had hurt another living thing. Many other stories tell of his gentle demeanor toward both the natural world and his devotees. Despite his best intentions, though, he too became embroiled in tensions with the Moguls, during the reign of Emperor Aurangzeb (1618–1707). It had been rumored that Guru Har Rai had favored Aurangzeb's elder brother, who was ultimately unsuccessful in succeeding Emperor Shah Jahan. Emperor Aurangzeb summoned Guru Har Rai to his court for questioning, but he sent instead his eldest son, Ram Rai, who was imprisoned by the emperor. Before Guru Har Rai died, at the age of thirty-one, he appointed his second son, Har Krishan (1656–1664), as his successor. Ram Rai eventually received the emperor's pardon and was offered revenue-free land in the Shivalik Hills, where, rejecting his younger brother's succession, he too started a center and gained a sizable following. When Guru Har Krishan died after three years, succumbing to the smallpox epidemic in the region, Ram Rai reasserted his claim to lead the Sikhs.

Historical evidence suggests the Moguls favored Ram Rai as Guru Har Rai's successor. Ram Rai also had a sizable following of Sikhs. Sikh narratives, however, tell of intrigue and Ram Rai's falling out of favor with his father. Emperor Aurangzeb, when Ram Rai was first brought before him, challenged the young man to explain a certain verse in the Sikh scriptures that appeared to slight Muslims. Ram Rai, it is said, changed its wording in such a way as not to antagonize the emperor. When Guru Har Rai heard of Ram Rai's alteration of scripture, he responded by appointing his youngest son, Har Krishan, guru, despite his being five years junior to Ram Rai.

While there is little historical basis for this latter version, the message of the story is clear. Given the growing power of rival gurus, particularly at the main center of Ramdaspur, the home of Harimandir Sahib and the Akal Takht, and their large followings, it was vital for the legitimate lineage of gurus to establish both its authority and the inviolability of their writings; the gurus' utterances were supreme, beyond challenge or alteration, even by the beloved son of a guru.

It is important to note that although the central issue of authentic succession divided these groups, there were few doctrinal differences between the mainstream community and these breakaway communities. All believed they were legitimate successors of Guru Nanak. They shared the same festivals, prayers, and rituals. Guru Nanak's discipline of *nam simran* was followed; the hymns of the early gurus were the mainstay of devotional life. Whereas a number of dissenters were avid poets and wrote a number of compositions, none of the legitimate gurus after Guru Arjan had added to the Kartarpur collection. This added considerably to the complexity of the question of authenticity in connection with the gurus' and their rivals' compositions.

Clearly, then, as now, there was not a single, homogeneous Sikh community. The legitimate and rival communities vied with one another for tithes and the loyalty of the deputies, the latter increasingly relied upon as Sikh territories continued to expand. Nonetheless, these various strands within the wider Sikh community for the most part lived harmoniously. Beyond the obvious differences arising over legitimate succession, there is no evidence of these tensions igniting into overt conflict.

Guru Tegh Bahadur

Guru Tegh Bahadur (1621–1675), the youngest son of Guru Hargobind, had been bypassed by his father as successor but succeeded his grand-nephew, the child guru Har Krishan, as the ninth guru. Traditional accounts reveal a flurry of rivalry over the succession of Guru Tegh Bahadur. Guru Har Krishan, as he lay dying, uttered the words "Baba Bakale"; it was thus believed that the ninth guru of the Sikhs would be found in the vicinity of the village of Bakala. The unforeseen response was that twenty-two claimants arrived in Bakala vying for the nomination. Given this predicament, an ingenious method, tradition tells, was invented for ascertaining the true guru. A merchant whose life had been spared at sea had earlier vowed that he would offer five hundred gold pieces to the legitimate guru. He subsequently announced that each claimant would instead receive a miniscule portion of the larger sum of gold, one or two pieces. He was convinced, however, that whoever insisted on the full amount would be the authentic master. According to Sikh tradition, Guru

Tegh Bahadur requested the remainder of the gold pieces, and so was nominated to succeed Guru Har Krishan.

After the considerable conflict over succession, Guru Tegh Bahadur did much to consolidate the Sikh community, visiting far-flung congregations and adding new hymns for use in the devotional life of the Sikhs. He invited poets to his court, and his own poetry lauded the bravery of those following the way of truth. Perhaps because of these compositions, near the end of Guru Tegh Bahadur's long life, the Moguls, interpreting the guru's message as a call for rebellion against the authorities, summoned him to Delhi. One account indicates a rival of Guru Tegh Bahadur's had registered a complaint against him. In 1675, he was charged with instigating rebellion against the government and executed.

Popular Sikh accounts give a different version of these events. Emperor Aurangzeb had decided that a group of Brahmins from Kashmir must convert to Islam. A deputation of these Brahmins came to Guru Tegh Bahadur, pleading with him to help. The guru challenged the emperor to instead attempt to convince *him* to convert. If the emperor succeeded, the Kashmir Brahmins too would become Muslims. If Aurangzeb failed, however, the Brahmins could continue to follow their own beliefs. Emperor Aurangzeb then demanded Guru Tegh Bahadur immediately convert to Islam. When the guru refused, he was summarily beheaded. The *gurdwara*, Sis Ganj, near where the execution occurred, is today an important pilgrimage site for Sikhs as well as many non-Sikhs. It commemorates the righteous act of sacrifice for the religious rights of all, including Hindu Brahmins. Regardless of whether or not this account is accurate, the ramifications of this second execution of one of the Sikh gurus were many. At the very least, relations between the Sikhs and Moguls further deteriorated.

Guru Gobind Singh

The succession of Gobind Rai, Guru Tegh Bahadur's only son, after his father's execution marked the beginning of a period of great change in the Sikh community. Guru Gobind Rai, later known as Guru Gobind Singh (1666–1708), succeeded his father at the young age of nine. He was trained in martial arts, was an avid hunter, and, according to accounts, was a superb horseman. The young guru had

Guru Gobind Singh, the tenth guru.
Courtesy of Kapany Collection of Sikh Art.

also been educated from an early age in court life and etiquette. He
studied foreign languages, astronomy, botany, and medicine. He was
also well versed in the diverse religious philosophies of India.

It was a tumultuous time for the Sikhs. Tensions had heightened
between the Moguls and the young guru as a result of his father's execution. There were also occasional confrontations between the guru's
army and Hindu rajas of the hill stations in the Shivalik Hills. Internal tensions were also rising as rival leaders vied for the loyalty of adherents and some of the guru's deputies began clamoring for power.

Guru Gobind Rai built a new center, Anandpur, complete with
four forts, one at each corner of the center's boundaries. Anandpur
flourished in the latter years of the seventeenth century. The new
center came to be known not only for its fortifications but also as a
literary and artistic center where poets and artists received the guru's
generous patronage. In addition, Guru Gobind Rai reclaimed Harimandir Sahib upon the death of one of his rivals, who had set up

court there when Guru Hargobind left the sacred site for the Shivalik
Hills, thus weakening rival control of Ramdaspur.

The Founding of the Khalsa

In 1699, during the Baisakhi New Year's celebrations, a time when
Sikhs gathered in great numbers, Guru Gobind Rai ordered all
Sikhs to join him at Anandpur. Ramdaspur, with its sacred shrine
and pool, was the traditional gathering place for Sikhs during festivals, and though the events surrounding this momentous event in
Sikh history are unknown, the guru's unusual call to his devotees to
gather at Anandpur was likely an effort to consolidate the Sikhs. As
the crowds gathered, Guru Gobind Rai suddenly called for a Sikh to
come forward to offer his head in devotion to his guru. The assembly
was stunned. Finally, one Sikh came forward. The guru then called
for four more, and four devoted Sikhs answered his call.

There are different accounts of what happened next. One tells of
the guru emerging from his tent with his sword dripping the blood
of the five devoted volunteers he had just sacrificed, only to then miraculously heal them. Another version has the guru sacrificing instead five goats as a ruse to test the will of his followers. Regardless of
the actual events, it is certain that the five disciples who stepped forward were given the label the five beloved ones *(panj piare)* and initiated into a new brotherhood. It is notable that each of the five came
from different castes. The names of these five devotees, Daya (Com-
passion), Dharm (Duty), Muhkam (Firmness), Himmat (Effort), and
Sahib (Honor), neatly echoed the main ideals first put in place by
Guru Nanak.

According to this new initiation ritual, called *khande di pahul*
(sword ritual), water sweetened with sugar was stirred in an iron
bowl with a double-edged sword. The guru then used his sword to
sprinkle this nectar over each initiate's face, cupped hands, eyes, and
hair a total of five times. Last, he offered them a confection *(karah
prasad)* specially prepared in an iron utensil and touched with the
tip of his sword. The initiates were henceforth members of what later
came to be known as the order of the Khalsa, a term used originally
by the Moguls to designate lands under the emperor's direct supervision. In the Sikh context, Khalsa referred to followers under the

direct authority of the guru as opposed to those under the guru's rivals. The former, and the guru himself, who also underwent the sword ritual, were given the name Singh (Lion); their master was thenceforth known as Guru Gobind Singh.

The earliest texts identify five weapons each Khalsa member was to carry. The five weapons apparently gave way to five essential identity markers Khalsas were to adopt, some of which included elements of a warrior's costume. They were a *kirpan* (dagger), a *kara* (steel bangle), worn to protect the sword-wielding right wrist, and *kachh* (short breeches), necessary to warriors for ease in mounting and dismounting their horses in times of battle. However, the injunctions also included an important focus on the body: *kesh,* uncut hair, represented the body in its pristine form, and the *kangha,* a small comb worn in the hair, emphasized tidiness and cleanliness. These five elements are known as the five *k*s *(panj kakar)*, each of the names of the symbols beginning with the letter *k*. The five *k*s, along with the turban for keeping the uncut hair in place, remain today as the distinctive marks of the Khalsa Sikh.

According to some sources, the guru also put in place at this time four rules of conduct, known as the *kurahits* (cardinal sins): Sikhs were forbidden to cut their hair, use tobacco or alcohol, and eat meat from animals slaughtered according to Muslim ritual. They were also to abstain from sexual relations with Muslim women. The latter injunctions clearly reflect the deteriorated relationship between Sikhs and Muslims during this time. The regulation was subsequently enlarged to prohibit adulterous relationships of any sort. The guru then called on others in the community to join the Khalsa order. According to tradition, great numbers came forward to join the order and thereby show their devotion to their guru. The office and authority of the deputies was also dissolved; tithes were to be brought directly to the guru at Anandpur, thus removing the possibility of intermediaries coming between Sikhs and their guru.

In this way, the Khalsa Sikhs were clearly set apart from their Hindu and Muslim counterparts as well as from the followers of rival gurus. They were henceforth to be known as a community of warrior-saints. Tradition is also clear that many Sikhs continued to follow the practices set down by the earlier gurus, rejecting the new markers associated with the Khalsa Sikhs. According to the earliest texts, women were not to be initiated into the order given that all those inaugurated were to be armed and ready for battle. Women thus stayed within the earlier definition of what it meant to be a Sikh.

Scholars have long struggled to understand the transformation of a developing Sikh tradition that at its inception stressed the interiority of true religion to one emphasizing, albeit *alongside* interior transformation, external manifestations of spirituality, namely, the external identifiers put in place by Guru Gobind Singh in the creation of the Khalsa. For many Sikhs, however, this is not difficult to comprehend. All the gurus acted according to the will of Akal Purakh. The divine light in Guru Nanak was the same light that shone equally brightly in each of the subsequent nine gurus. Each made decisions based on differing social and political forces. The creation of the Khalsa was simply a righteous and divinely ordained response to the machinations of the Mogul rulers who were determined to weaken the Sikh community. According to this perspective, it is possible that had Guru Gobind Singh not created the Khalsa identity setting Sikhs apart from other religions, Sikhism would likely not have flourished.

Although scholars do not necessarily discount the workings of the Divine throughout Sikh history, attempts are made to bring additional perspectives to bear to explain the changes that took place in the developing community. Perhaps most important, Guru Nanak's insistence on the householder as an ideal had paved the way for an understanding of the inseparableness of the temporal and the spiritual. Guru Nanak's meditative discipline allowed followers to be fully present to the everyday aspects of life, domestic and political, at the same time remembering the divine name and becoming attuned to the will of Akal Purakh. The institutionalization of the community, which included a more complex role of the guru as both spiritual and political authority, the collation of the orally transmitted hymns into a scriptural text, the establishment of sacred sites of pilgrimage, and the dispatch of emissaries proclaiming the message of the gurus also had vital roles in the development of a community set apart from the wider society. Moreover, the political situation had changed dramatically from the time of Guru Nanak to that of Guru Gobind

Singh. The Mogul authorities had become ever more doubtful of the political loyalty of their Sikh subjects. An important element of Mogul opprobrium evolved around changes in the composition of the Sikh community, which had gradually transformed from a primarily Khatri-based membership at its inception to one dominated by the Jat caste. Scholars suggest it is highly likely that the Sikh community was developing in response to the character and conventions of this ever more powerful group. Considering that Jats were closely associated with martial traditions, the institutionalization of the warrior-saint ideal at Anandpur may well be tied to an earlier absorption of Jat cultural practices within the wider community. However, Guru Gobind Singh's creation of the Khalsa order was also an attempt to unify an increasingly splintered community; those bearing the signs of the Khalsa brotherhood made it clear to all they were the true devotees of the one and only true guru.

The Sikhs after Guru Gobind Singh

The Moguls were alarmed by this militant turn in the Sikh community. Two elder sons of Guru Gobind Singh died fighting in a battle against Mogul forces; his two youngest sons were later executed, and the guru's mother, Mata Gujuri, died in a Mogul prison. The guru was heartbroken and wrote a letter of admonishment, known by the name Zafarnama, to Emperor Aurangzeb recounting the cruelty of the Mogul governor of the region and his forces. The emperor responded by inviting the guru to meet him, but before they could meet, Aurangzeb died. Emperor Bahadur Shah, who succeeded Aurangzeb, had earlier been blessed by Guru Gobind Singh in the battle of succession against one of his brothers. Guru Gobind Singh was invited to accompany the new emperor to the south of India on a diplomatic mission, where, however, the guru was assassinated, in 1708, in the town of Nander, in present-day Maharashtra.

Since all Guru Gobind Singh's sons had been killed, there was no one within the guru lineage to lead the Sikhs after him. Many historians believe that for this reason, before his death, Guru Gobind Singh formally ended the institution of guruship. Other narratives point instead to divine revelation behind this development. Regardless, from this juncture Sikh authority resided in what was henceforth known as the Guru Granth Sahib, the sacred scripture of the Sikhs, as well as in the *guru panth,* the Sikh community. The day-to-day leadership of the Sikhs was to be based in the local congregation, led by an executive body modeled on the five beloved ones who had offered their heads in response to their guru's initial call. The congregation was to be further guided by the wisdom and insight of the Guru Granth Sahib. This form of leadership is still followed by Sikhs worldwide.

Banda Bahadur

While Guru Gobind Singh was in southern India with Emperor Bahadur Shah, he met an ascetic known as Madho Das, who became a disciple of the guru's. Keenly aware of the political and internal struggles among the Moguls and the potential for conflict, and recognizing Madho Das' leadership qualities, he renamed him Banda Bahadur (Brave Servant) and sent him ahead to Punjab to begin organizing the Sikhs. Because Banda Bahadur was the last bearer of the guru's commands, he was received as the new warrior chief of the Sikhs upon the news of Guru Gobind Singh's death. Banda Bahadur led a number of successful uprisings against the Moguls, but he too was soon overcome by the massive Mogul army and executed in 1716, and the authorities began in earnest on a campaign to exterminate the Khalsa Sikhs. But the Moguls themselves had been weakened by repeated Afghan invasions from the north led by Ahmad Shah Abdali. Abdali's army also targeted the Sikhs in an attempt to overcome all resistance. It was thus a time of intense persecution of the Sikhs. The noble Sikh heroes who resisted the Moguls and Afghans are still named and honored in Sikh prayers of remembrance on a daily basis as the greatest of Sikh martyrs. The ideal of martyrdom became firmly entrenched in the Sikh psyche, understood then as now as a righteous fight to the death, of the upholding of faith in the face of intolerance and persecution.

The Sikh Confederacy Period, Maharajah Ranjit Singh, and the Fall of the Sikh Empire

By the mid-eighteenth century, independent Sikh confederacies were being organized under the leadership of a commanding chief. The twelve confederacies were especially skilled in guerrilla warfare against the Afghan army. As a body, these armies were known as the Army of the Khalsa; when the confederacies gathered together, they were known as the Sarbat Khalsa (Entire Khalsa). The Sarbat Khalsa took on added significance inasmuch as any decisions taken in accordance with Sikh scripture were claimed to be *gurmata,* or the "will of the guru," and were binding upon all members. In time, however, the confederacies themselves began waging war on one another in an attempt to gain ascendancy.

Through his own political astuteness, but also under the guidance of his equally ambitious mother-in-law, Maharani Sada Kaur, Ranjit Singh soon rose to prominence. Under Maharajah Ranjit Singh and after the consolidation of his kingdom, Punjab entered four decades (1801–1849) of relative peace and prosperity. It is a time remembered as one of Sikh glory, for although the Sikhs were a small minority in the surrounding sea of Hindus and Muslims, it was a Sikh who ruled a significant portion of northern India. Following Maharajah Ranjit Singh's death, however, it became clear that his numerous heirs did not have the same leadership qualities as their father. Following two Anglo-Sikh wars (1845–1846 and 1848–1849), the Sikh kingdom became the final area annexed by the British, in 1849. From this point onward, the British ruled over the entire Indian subcontinent. The Sikhs fared well, the Raj grudgingly admiring the leadership of Maharajah Ranjit Singh and the military prowess of his armies. Having pledged their loyalty to their new rulers, Sikhs were given considerable autonomy, offered educational initiatives, and welcomed into the British Army. The Sikh aristocracy and religious elite were offered land grants and special rights to ensure their loyalty to the British crown.

The Singh Sabha Reform Movement

As in other parts of India, religio-political reform movements in Punjab sprang up as a British-educated, elite middle-class began reevaluating deeply rooted religious beliefs and practices in the context of the new political landscape put in place by the British. The Sikh Singh Sabha reform movement was initiated in the late nineteenth century. There were two main groups in this movement. The first was centered in Amritsar and was known as the Amritsar Singh

Sabha. This group was composed largely of prominent Sikhs, including members of the religious elite and the aristocracy. They represented the pinnacle of Sikh society and included many members and leaders who adhered to highly inclusive beliefs and practices that drew widely from surrounding Hindu traditions, often designated as Sanatan Sikhism. The second faction was based in Lahore. This group called itself Tat Khalsa (True Khalsa) and stood for what it believed to be a purer and exclusively Khalsa-oriented interpretation of Sikh identity. A number of lower-caste Sikhs had important positions in the Lahore Sabha. Members of this group began chafing at their treatment by the elitist members in the Amritsar faction, which the Lahore group believed was far too lax in upholding true Sikh tenets. The disputes between these two factions were often fierce, but in the end the Lahore Singh Sabha came to dominate reform efforts. The movement was on the whole loyal to the British, for it was as a result of British or Christian missionary educational initiatives that many Sikhs of the lower castes had acquired middle-class status.

The Tat Khalsa reforms under the umbrella of the larger Singh Sabha movement had far-reaching results, especially in relation to their efforts to redefine and explain the essence of Sikhism in a manner that befitted the values and worldview of this educated elite. Members of the Singh Sabha were greatly influenced by Christian missionary techniques and by their British masters' criticism of Indian religious practices. Earlier, orientalist scholars had undertaken to discover the "pure" teachings of the dominant religions of India. Religious practices that did not fit into the orientalists' rigid understanding of unadulterated religious observances were negatively labeled as mere superstition or simply as the popular customs of the illiterate masses. In this context, many Indian religious reform movements, including the Singh Sabha, assumed a similar view of many popular religious practices. Many were labeled by the Singh Sabha as irrational, superstitious, and anti-Sikh elements that had come from surrounding belief systems. An important aspect of Singh Sabha reform thus focused on distinguishing Sikhs from the practices, rituals, and attitudes of Hindus and Muslims in particular. In rural Punjab, where the majority of Sikhs resided (as now), the populace tended to share many of the festivals, shrines, and religious practices of those around them. While the Khalsa ideal had gained ascendancy, other varieties of Sikh identity were also prevalent in the late nineteenth and early twentieth centuries. Among them were the ascetic, scholarly Sikhs known as Udasis, the Namdhari, and the Nirankari Sikhs, groups that, though following the major Sikh tenets, also upheld a tradition of guru lineages. Many Sikhs were followers of revered guru lineages, some from the various rival groups of the early guru period. Others simply rejected the Khalsa identity while upholding the beliefs and practices of the earlier gurus.

Nonetheless, the Tat Khalsa reforms ultimately came to represent what we know as Sikhism today. This was due mainly to Tat Khalsa reformers' understanding of the importance of the printing press, introduced to Punjab by Christian missionaries. Many members of the Lahore Singh Sabha, educated in missionary schools, had first-hand experience with the methods and practices of the Christian missionary establishment. They included the cheap, quick production of tracts and newspapers used by the missionaries for spreading the Christian message. As a new middle class of doctors, lawyers, teachers, journalists, and government officials, these reformers also understood and thoroughly embraced the usefulness of the printed word. This development also brought substantive changes in the power dynamics of the Sikhs. The power traditionally held by the highly conservative religious and political aristocracy, largely dependent on oral communication, shifted to the new elite that controlled the printed word, and also claimed to more fully represent Sikh political and religious interests. According to Harjot Oberoi, these

> elites were new not so much [so] in terms of their social origins but in their social functions, and, more importantly, in the instruments of transmission they appropriated. . . . They were emerging as a power bloc the like of which had never existed before in northern India. In pre-British society there had never been one social group that enjoyed the sole rights to generate cultural meanings and define people's lives. . . . But in colonial Punjab, during the second half of the nineteenth century, there emerged a restless new elite that cut across kin ties, neighbourhood networks and even caste affiliations. (Oberoi 1994, 264–265)

Tat Khalsa reformers promoted a single Sikh identity, that of the Khalsa Sikhs. To ensure that Sikh practices clearly stood apart from Hindu and Muslim rites, novel rituals and festivals were developed and presented as distinctively Sikh. In addition, Sikhism was presented as a thoroughly modern and egalitarian tradition. Reformers opened the Khalsa sword ritual to Sikh women. They also offered Sikh women a name analogous to that of Singh to distinguish them from Muslim and Hindu women, namely Kaur. Sikhs who participated in non-Sikh religious festivals were roundly criticized in newspapers as promoting "un-Sikh" behavior and blamed for what reformers perceived as the highly degenerate state of Sikhism. Sikh centers of education and the popular media were put to use for the creation of a new, reformed vision and understanding of a distinct, homogeneous Sikh identity. Many of these changes of Sikh identity and practices instituted by the Singh Sabha continue to characterize the Sikh tradition.

The Sikhs and Politics in the Early Twentieth Century

Across India, the call for Indian independence from British rule grew more strident. Sikhs too, though for the most part loyal to the British, began raising their voices against foreign rule. This was particularly the case after 1919, when an incident took place in Amritsar known as the Jallianwala Bagh (Park) Massacre. Following days of protest and general unrest over British policies, in April that year, Brigadier General Dyer placed Amritsar under martial law. The annual Baisakhi festival had brought large numbers of Sikhs to Amritsar, many gathered at Jallianwala Bagh, near Harimandir Sahib. Under Dyer's command, riflemen began firing into the enclosed area, and, although the exact numbers are not known, official records indicate that 379 individuals were killed and many more wounded in the assault. Most of the victims were Sikhs. This incident added considerable psychological support for the Quit India Movement and increased anti-British sentiment among the Sikhs.

In 1920, the Shiromani Gurdwara Parbandhak Committee (SGPC) and the Shiromani Akali Dal were formed. Collectively they were known as the Akalis, Akal meaning "Timeless One," a common Sikh name for the Divine. The Akalis had political aspirations but as an explicitly Sikh movement also offered a strong measure of religious authority in representing Sikhs in the early 1920s. After a number of years of mainly peaceful protest against British interference in Sikh religious affairs and successful political organizing, the Sikh Gurdwara Act was passed in 1925. The act gave the administration of the *gurdwaras* and shrines in the state of Punjab to the Sikhs through the governing SGPC, thus removing control from the hereditary proprietors of these shrines, who had operated with the support of the British. SGPC oversight of the shrines also included Harimandir Sahib, representing an important victory for reformist Sikhs. Until the early years of the twentieth century, certain rituals and practices had taken place in the temple that were in direct opposition to the views and beliefs of reform-oriented Sikhs. In 1905, for instance, reformers had removed a number of Hindu statues from the Harimandir Sahib compound; the hereditary proprietors of the shrine did not make the same distinctions between Hindu and Sikh practices and beliefs as did the reformers. With the 1925 Sikh Gurdwara Act, Khalsa Sikhs could appoint their own managers of the *gurdwaras* and thus exert greater control over what took place within their sacred shrines.

World War II, Indian Independence, and Partition

World War II temporarily stemmed the tide of the movement for Indian independence. Sikhs played an important and brave part in the war not only as citizens of the Crown but also as a disproportionately large contingent in the Indian Army. The British had long nurtured what they believed to be the innate martial spirit of the Sikhs.

Closely following the end of World War II, on August 15, 1947, at the stroke of midnight, India gained independence from British rule. Yet the independence so sorely won after the many years of agitation against imperial rule came at a great price for millions of Indians. With Indian independence also came the partitioning of India, resulting in great swathes of the country being divided between India and the newly formed nation of Pakistan. The state of Bengal was also divided, its eastern portion becoming East Pakistan. The years of violence in the region did not end with partition; after the Indo-Pakistani War of 1971, East Pakistan seceded and became the independent nation of Bangladesh.

A number of princely states, nominally sovereign entities outside British rule, were excluded from the Independence Act of 1947. Each Indian ruler then had to choose whether to join India or Pakistan. One such state was Jammu and Kashmir. At the time of partition, the state was mainly Muslim in population. Its leader, Maharajah Har Singh, originally refused to join either Pakistan or India, choosing instead to remain independent. In 1948, Pakistan sought control over the state, but Singh then ceded the state to India. Today, Pakistan and India both claim control of the region, and it continues to be a site of tense conflict.

Punjab, homeland of the Sikhs, was split into East and West Punjab. East Punjab went to India, and West Punjab became part of Pakistan, despite the insistence by many Muslims that all of Punjab be handed over to Pakistan. Master Tara Singh (1885–1967) and other Sikh leaders, unlike Muslims under the leadership of Muhammad Ali Jinnah (1876–1948), were unable to make the case for a separate Sikh state.

These great shifts in control led to a mass exodus of millions of Sikhs and Hindus leaving their homelands for the newly defined state of India and of Muslims for Pakistan. Major riots accompanied this mass migration, leading to massacres on both sides of the new borders. The exact number of casualties from the violence at the time is not known, although figures range as high as 1.5 million. As a community, the Sikhs suffered greatly from the partition in light of the huge number of those affected by the resettlement process. Partition meant leaving behind Lahore, the erstwhile capital of the Sikh kingdom of Maharajah Ranjit Singh, their homes, their livelihoods, and their ancestral villages. Perhaps most tragically for Sikhs, many of the holy sites, shrines, and *gurdwaras* associated with the Sikh gurus fell within the borders of Pakistan.

Punjabi Suba and the Anandpur Sahib Resolution

Another important political milestone was reached by the Sikhs in 1966 as a result of the Punjabi Suba movement. Led by the Shiromani Akali Dal political party, the movement's aim was the creation of a Sikh state with Punjabi and Gurmukhi as the official language and script. Before 1966, Sikhs had constituted just over 33 percent of Punjab;

after 1966, they made up a majority at 60 percent of the population. This shift resulted from parts of Punjab being divided between two other states, Haryana and Himachal Pradesh, both with Hindu majorities. The city of Chandigarh served, as today, as the capital of both Haryana and Punjab, with Sikhs retaining their majority status in Punjab.

In 1966 the Shiromani Akali Dal was able to form the government of Punjab, but by 1972 the Congress Party had again gained control of the Punjab Assembly. In an attempt to consolidate its position, the Akali Dal passed a declaration in 1973, the Anandpur Sahib Resolution, seeking to limit the role and power of the central government and calling for increased autonomy for Sikhs and the state of Punjab. Although the resolution was rejected by the central government, the efforts and aspirations behind it continue to influence Punjabi politics.

The 1980s to the Present

Sikh grievances against the central government and perceived economic and political discrimination persisted into the 1980s. In 1981, there was a demand for an independent Sikh state, to be called Khalistan. The militant political and religious leader Sant Jarnail Singh Bhindranwale (1947–1984) called for a new nation governed by Sikhs and built upon Khalsa ideals. Bhindranwale and his followers urged Sikhs to reject all identities except that of the Khalsa Sikhs. They also called for a return to the combined spiritual and political authority of Sikhs introduced by Guru Hargobind, symbolized by the two swords *miri* and *piri* and Harimandir Sahib and the Akal Takht. Bhindranwale's vision also stemmed from his interpretation of Guru Gobind Singh's call to militancy for the sake of righteousness.

The central government under Prime Minister Indira Gandhi (1917–1984), the daughter of Jawaharlal Nehru, independent India's first prime minister, became alarmed by Bhindranwale's growing power in Punjab. In late 1983 Bhindranwale and a group of followers occupied the Akal Takht armed with not only the traditional sword but also modern weapons. When the Indian Army attacked, on June 5, 1984, Harimandir Sahib in an effort to flush out Bhindranwale and his followers, one of the most painful episodes of modern

Sikh history occurred. The attack on their sacred shrine and killing of their spiritual and political leader outraged the Sikh community. The significance of the date of the assault, the anniversary of
Guru Arjan's death at the hands of the Moguls, was not lost on the
Sikhs. This woke many Sikhs to the erosion of their religious and
political rights by India's government and military; Sikhs who had
not joined the Khalistani movement now aligned themselves with
its objectives.

Political tensions intensified after two Sikh bodyguards assassinated Gandhi on October 31, 1984, in revenge for her decision to send
troops into the Harimandir Sahib complex. Some members of the
Hindu community promised revenge in return. Mobs in Delhi and
in other Indian cities began roaming the streets, especially in areas
with large numbers of Sikhs. Many Sikh homes and businesses were
burned to the ground, and thousands of Sikhs, outwardly recognizable as such, were brutally attacked. In Delhi alone some three thousand died at the hands of rioting mobs.

The Sikh community was shocked by the violence and sobered
by the realization of the precariousness of their situation as a tiny
minority beside the two larger religious affiliations in India. Hindus constitute about 80 percent of the population, Muslims around
13 percent, with Sikhs composing less than 2 percent.

The subsequent years were a time of political and religious uncer-
tainty for Sikhs both in India and in the Sikh diaspora; it was a time
of intense reevaluation of Sikh identity. Although much of the former anguish has subsided, especially in Punjab, in some Sikh communities outside India, particularly in Canada and the United Kingdom, the dream of an independent Khalistan has continued to be
nurtured. Nonetheless, the number of Sikhs who support this radical
initiative has rapidly dwindled. Punjab has long returned to an or-
derly state with Sikhs, Hindus, and Muslims living in peaceful coexistence. The year 2004 was a turning point for many Sikhs around
the world. Dr. Manmohan Singh, a renowned economist and politi-
cian, and a turbaned Sikh, was sworn in as India's fourteenth prime
minister. The election of a member of a tiny minority to India's highest political office has been significant for all other minority groups
in India, in particular of course for Sikhs.

CHAPTER 3

Sikh Beliefs, Institutions, and Rituals

Central to Sikh teachings is the belief in the oneness of God. Yet the Sikh gurus used a variety of names for the divine from both the Hindu and Muslim traditions. Common names for the Ultimate used by the gurus included Formless One, Nirgun, and Akal Purakh, Eternal Being. According to their teachings, Akal Purakh is manifest in the world as well as within the human heart. From this perspective, Akal Purakh can be understood as both having and not having attributes. Guru Gobind Singh's Khalsa order ushered in another representation of divinity, Sarab Loh (All Steel), the burnished steel of the unsheathed sword. Another term that became central to the Sikh conception of divinity is Vahiguru (Wonderful Sovereign). Worth noting is that Sikhism does not subscribe to polytheistic understandings of the Divine.

Like the Bhakti poet-saints, the gurus described the striving for union with the Divine in terms of the joys of marital bliss. A true devotee of the Divine was often presented as the bride of Akal Purakh.

> The Sikh Gurus often invoke the classic imagery of separation and fusion between the lover and the beloved: the virgin bride who anticipates the embrace of the bridegroom on her wedding night, or the wife's longing for her husband's return from a far-off land. Bride, wife and virgin are metaphors for the self which is individuated and which pines for union with the other which is divine. The re-joining of the two is the Absolute as One. (Shackle and Mandair 2005, xxix)

The gurus also taught that while the essence of Akal Purakh is beyond human comprehension, that essence is everywhere, in every object, experience, and relationship. It is noteworthy that the gurus did
not refer to Akal Purakh exclusively in masculine terms, conceiving
more broadly of God as father or mother, sister or brother.

The Human Condition

According to Sikh thought, humans have an innate connection with
Akal Purakh. Guru Nanak referred to the human soul as emanating
from the light of God. For this reason, humanity is essentially good.
But there is a "problem" with the human condition: humans do not
recognize that their true essence emanates from God. Human beings are unaware that the presence of God is in them and surrounds
them at all times. This problem, what the Gurus called *haumai,* is a
reliance on the self in the absence of a recognition of one's ultimate
dependence on God. Humans are also *manmukh,* bound to the ego
and centered on the self. This concept is related to *maya* (illusion). In
Sikhism *maya* is associated with worldly attachment, a materialis-
tic view of the world. As such, one lives in a delusional state. Though
attachment to one's child, home, or job is not necessarily evil, when
combined with *haumai,* attachment may take on negative qualities.
Sikhs speak of five major evils, among many other lesser ones. They
are lust, covetousness or greed, attachment, wrath, and pride. *Maya*
is love turned into possessiveness. *Maya* is the God-given attraction
to another perverted to lust.

The gurus taught that the destiny of each individual is directly
tied to actions from past lives as well as those of the present. This is
known in the wider Indian philosophical and religious systems as
karma. This notion is related to transmigration, the cycle of birth,
death, and rebirth resulting from one's karma. Whereas being born
as a human is understood as a great privilege, rebirth can also take
place in the form of an animal or insect. However, faithfully practicing the discipline of *nam simran* and loving devotion of Akal
Purakh, in other words, becoming increasingly attuned to the divine
will, can overcome the bonds of karma and for release from the wea-
risome circle of rebirth.

But the gurus did not only address the human condition but also offered a hopeful and clear solution to the human predicament. The goal, they taught, is to move away from reliance on the self and on the ego to a constant focus on Akal Purakh. The direct path to liberation is the practice of *nam simran.* By focusing on Vahiguru in everyday living, humans and the Divine will begin to converge. The gurus did not mean one must give up one's occupation and house and family; *nam simran* can and should be practiced within the ordinary course of daily life. While sowing the fields, mending, churning butter, all images used by the gurus, one can participate in the discipline of meditation. Congregational singing of praises to Akal Purakh is also essential in the spiritual quest, for in being in the company of like-minded people, all striving for union with Akal Purakh, the personal quest for liberation is enhanced.

The gurus taught that there are five stages *(khand)* through which humans must pass before attaining liberation. The first stage into which all humans are born is *dharam khand,* the stage of duty or piety. In this stage, humans act according to notions of duty based on basic levels of responsibility and piety. In practicing devotion, they are enabled to reach the second stage, *gyan khand,* the realm of awareness or knowledge. This awareness is based on a deeper under-standing of reality, one that goes beyond simple actions for the sake of duty. In this stage, devotees become aware of the mystery of Akal Purakh and the vastness of the universe. The realm of effort, *saram khand,* is the next stage, in which the mind and intellect become more and more attuned to Akal Purakh. This stage is also the last in-volving human effort and insight. While Vahiguru's gift of grace per-meates all stages of liberation, movement to the fourth stage, known as the stage of grace, or *karam khand,* entails a direct response from the Divine to an individual's sincere striving. In other words, karam khand is possible only by Vahiguru's gift of grace. Through grace, the seeker finds peace, having realized the true meaning of life, namely, that the essence of Akal Purakh is the same essence of one's true self. The last stage is the realm of truth, *sach khand,* the realm where the essence of Nirgun exists, formless and everlasting. This realm can-not be described; it can only be experienced. At this stage the *gur-mukh* no longer perceives the world from a human perspective but from the perspective of Akal Purakh. This is true liberation and the end of the spiritual quest. Liberation can be achieved in the present life, *jiwan mukti* (living liberation), not only in death. The individual who has attained *sach khand* no longer experiences the negative effects of karma and the cycle of birth and death. The cycle of transmigration is broken and the seeker finally rests in absolute union with Akal Purakh upon her or his death.

Sikh Religious Practices: The Three Cornerstones

When asked to summarize what is primary to Sikhism and how the gurus' teachings translate into their daily lives, Sikhs often point to what has been characterized as the three cornerstones of Sikhism: first, remembrance of Vahiguru at all times through the discipline of *nam simran,* including congregational singing and prayer; second, working honestly without exploitation or fraud based on the householder ideal put in place by Guru Nanak (in opposition to a life of asceticism and begging for one's daily food); and third, sharing with others and helping those in need.

Sikh Worship

THE *GURDWARA*

The term *gurdwara* gradually replaced the term *dharmsala* as the Sikh community developed, particularly from the time of Guru Hargobind, who built numerous *gurdwaras* as special sites associated with earlier gurus. *Gurdwaras* can be found in all parts of the world today; most are recognizable by the triangular saffron flag, called a Nishan Sahib, fluttering high on a saffron flagpole beside the building.

On the flag is the Sikh symbol of the *khanda,* the Khalsa emblem of the double-edged sword. Of all *gurdwaras,* the most sacred is Harimandir Sahib in Amritsar.

The Guru Granth Sahib is the focal point of every *gurdwara.* While devotional singing and readings are taken from the text, all ceremonies and rituals must also take place in its physical presence. In the *gurdwara* (as in many Sikh homes), the Guru Granth Sahib, the living guru of the Sikhs, is accorded the respect and dignity due royalty. When the Guru Granth Sahib as the living guru of the Sikhs is ritually awakened in its nightly resting place, an elaborate

*Nishan Sahib displayed at Makindu Gurdwara,
Makindu, Kenya. Courtesy of Karam Bharij.*

bed placed in a separate room, it is reverently carried on the head of
a devout Sikh to the main hall of the *gurdwara* accompanied by devotees waiting to receive its blessings. The Guru Granth Sahib is then
enthroned on a majestic seat of embroidered cushions and wrapped
in robes under an elaborate canopy. These ritual acts ensure that
those assembled understand that they are being granted an audience with a scripture that is accorded the spiritual authority of a living guru. When entering the main hall of the *gurdwara* where the
Guru Granth Sahib is enthroned, devotees bow low and touch their
foreheads to the ground, and only then are they ready to take part in
congregational devotional activities.

Swedish scholar Kristina Myrvold beautifully explains the development of these ritual acts of devotion toward the Guru Granth Sahib:

> As believing Sikhs interpret their history, the Guru Granth Sa-
> hib came to manifest the "spirit" of all the ten historical Gurus
> and enshrine the total divine knowledge and power revealed to
> humanity by its predecessors. Devotional stances which Sikh be-
> lievers had taken toward the human Gurus of the past would like-
> wise be taken to the scripture. With the shift of authority the same

ethos and modes of practice that presumably existed in the courtly and domestic culture of the human Gurus were to be applied in contexts in which Sikh believers interacted with the Guru Granth Sahib. As a consequence, the scripture was attributed habits of human culture, and to be made the subject of various Sikh devotional practices. . . . The careful ministrations of the Sikh scripture must be viewed from the perspective of enduring devotional and social relationships between Sikh disciples and a scripture invested with spiritual authority. Well aware that the Guru Granth Sahib is a book made of paper and ink, and not alive in any physical sense, Sikhs treat the text as if it possessed the social agency of a personal Guru who continues to communicate divine knowledge and mediates human relationships. . . . By tradition the scriptural form of the Guru Granth Sahib requires the same respectful treatment as was given to the living human Gurus. Through reciting and singing hymns of the scripture the Sikhs are constantly mediating and making present the true agency or "spirit" of the guru embodied in the text. (Myrvold 2008, 142–143)

Also primary in congregational worship is the singing of devotional hymns. Daily congregational worship is prescribed in the Sikh Reht Maryada. Although any adult Sikh, male or female, can lead services in a *gurdwara,* they are generally conducted by a male *granthi* (custodian or reader of scripture) of the *gurdwara.* The term *granthi* is often translated as "priest," but that is misleading since there is no established and trained priesthood in the Sikh tradition. Other important roles in *gurdwara* life are fulfilled by trained musicians called *ragis* who sing the hymns accompanied by an instrument known as a harmonium and by the tabla, a small Indian percussion instrument.

The harmonium is a relatively new addition to Sikh worship. It was introduced to India by Christian missionaries, who used the simple instrument in congregations that did not have an organ to accompany their hymns. The harmonium is a keyboard instrument with bellows that are pumped by hand; it has largely replaced other instruments historically important in Sikh worship music, although efforts are currently under way to revive ancient stringed instruments for use in Sikh worship.

Ragis *at Gurdwara Sis Ganj, Delhi. Courtesy of Karam Bharij.*

Once the Guru Granth Sahib has been enthroned, morning services begin with the recital and singing of specific Sikh prayers and hymns. They conclude with the recitation of the *ardas* (prayer of remembrance) by the *granthi* while congregants stand quietly with folded hands. A randomly chosen hymn known as a divine order from scripture is read and a special confection *(karah prasad)* is then distributed to all who are assembled, irrespective of their caste or creed. Additional services occur throughout the day until nighttime, when the Guru Granth Sahib is carried to its royal resting place, to be awakened again with the breaking of the morning light.

Sikhs warmly welcome visitors to their *gurdwaras*. When entering, shoes must be removed and a covering must be placed on one's head as a traditional sign of respect to the Guru Granth Sahib. Women generally wear a light scarf; unturbaned men wear a small kerchief. Tobacco is not permitted in a *gurdwara* since its presence would be construed as highly disrespectful of the Sikh understanding of tobacco use as one of the four cardinal sins.

Upon entering the main hall that houses the sacred scripture, Sikhs touch the palms of their hands together as a sign of devotion, then walk toward the Guru Granth Sahib, which is kept on a raised, canopied platform supported by cushions and beautiful cloth. The *granthi,* seated in front of the Guru Granth Sahib, slowly waves a whisk over the scripture, a tradition rooted in shielding royal personages from insects. Once before the Guru Granth Sahib, Sikhs kneel, touch the forehead to the ground, and then make an offering of money or food. The hall is divided according to gender. Males sit on the right and females sit on the left. Younger children may sit on either side. Any visitor to the *gurdwara* is welcome to take part in this act of devotion; otherwise, a guest may simply join in by entering the hall with folded hands and sitting quietly during the service.

Some Sikhs visit the *gurdwara* daily but may simply enter the main hall, kneel before the Guru Granth Sahib, and then leave; others sit for the entire service. Most of the service consists of the singing of hymns but also includes a sermon by the *granthi* or another respected and devout Sikh male. The service comes to an end with the solemn recitation of the closing prayer, followed by communal chanting of the Sikh salutations: *Vahiguru ka Khalsa, Vahiguru ki fateh* (Hail to the guru's Khalsa! Hail to the guru's victory) and *Sat Sri Akal* (Truth is immortal). At the end of the service, the confection is distributed to all. This puddinglike sweet made of flour, sugar, and butter is received in cupped hands, left over right, then eaten with the right hand. After leaving the main hall, everyone is invited to a simple but delicious vegetarian meal *(langar)*. While the majority of Sikhs are not vegetarian, food offered at the *gurdwara* must be vegetarian. This tradition has been upheld so that the needs of those who are strictly vegetarian, both Sikhs and non-Sikhs, can be met. In India and in most *gurdwaras* in the Sikh diaspora, this meal is eaten while sitting within marked lines on the floor and is served by members of the congregation, male or female. In some areas of the Sikh diaspora this meal is eaten while seated at a table.

PERSONAL WORSHIP

The daily routine of a Sikh begins with rising early, bathing, and then reciting specific hymns from the Guru Granth Sahib. There are also prescribed hymns to be sung at sunset and just before bedtime. Many Sikh households, whether in India or in other parts of the world, have a special room reserved for a copy of the Guru Granth Sahib. This room serves as the family *gurdwara*. Whether the *gurdwara* is public or private, the Guru Granth Sahib must be treated with utmost respect and devotion.

Sikh Festivals and Celebrations

Throughout the Sikh world, the Baisakhi festival heralds Guru Gobind Singh's inauguration of the Khalsa in 1699. It also marks the New Year's celebrations as one agricultural cycle ends and another begins. Although the grandest celebration takes place in Amritsar, Baisakhi is celebrated at *gurdwaras* the world over. On this day, the triangular flag is washed and the old saffron-colored cloths wrapping the pole are removed and replaced by new ones. The Guru Granth Sahib is taken from the *gurdwara* and paraded around the town or city in a procession called the Nagar Kirtan, with the five beloved ones leading the procession either on foot or on horseback. Singing devotional hymns, the gathered congregation follows in great numbers. Traditionally, Baisakhi is also the time when Sikhs are initiated into the Khalsa order.

Baisakhi Nagar Kirtan procession, Coventry, UK.
Courtesy of Karam Bharij.

The Indian festival of Diwali, known as the festival of lights, is celebrated by Sikhs instead to honor the release of Guru Hargobind from Gwalior prison by Emperor Jahangir. When the guru finally arrived at Harimandir Sahib, he was welcomed by his devotees there, who had decorated it with lights. Today at Diwali Harimandir Sahib is decked with lights and a massive display of fireworks, to the delight of onlookers. This celebration also takes place in *gurdwaras* in other parts of the world.

The festival of Hola Mohalla, similar to the Sikh celebration of Diwali, has been lent a specific Sikh meaning as compared with the Hindu spring festival of Holi. It celebrates the summoning of Sikhs by Guru Gobind Singh to Anandpur at the inauguration of the Khalsa order. Sikhs celebrate Hola Mohalla at Anandpur with martial arts competitions called *gatka,* which include ancient weaponry like swords, bows and arrows, and chains. The festival also features other sporting events and weapons training exercises.

Gurpurbs celebrate important anniversaries in the history of Sikhism. The most widely celebrated *gurpurbs* include the birthdays of Guru Nanak and Guru Gobind Singh, as well as the martyrdom anniversary of Guru Arjan, the fifth guru. These special days are usually marked by processions headed by the Guru Granth Sahib along specific routes within cities or towns and accompanied by music and singing. Speeches by prominent individuals are also often part of the celebrations.

Central Sikh Institutions: Harimandir Sahib

Harimandir Sahib, also known as the Golden Temple, or Darbar Sahib, is the main shrine of the Sikhs. It is not only their most sacred place of worship but also a potent symbol of the heritage of the Sikhs throughout their five-hundred-year history and of the philosophy of the Sikh gurus. Guru Ram Das founded the city of Amritsar and excavated a pool that was believed to have healing properties as a place of pilgrimage for the developing Sikh community. Guru Arjan planned and built a *gurdwara* in the center of the pool and installed within it a completed version of the Sikh scripture of that time, the writings of the first four gurus as well as his own compositions.

While traditionally Hindu temples are built on a higher level than surrounding structures, the guru had the Harimandir Sahib built on a lower level so that devotees would have to go down steps in order to worship. One explanation for this change is the Sikh emphasis on humility. Another distinguishing feature of Harimandir Sahib is that instead of the traditional single point of entry as in most temples, the shrine is open on all four sides, representing entry to all regardless of caste or wealth.

Harimandir was repeatedly destroyed by invaders and assumed its present form during the confederacy period of Sikh history in the early eighteenth century. At this time it came to be called the Golden Temple, reflecting the gilding of the upper stories of the shrine done under the auspices of Maharajah Ranjit Singh.

Sikh Emblems and Symbols

IK OANKAR AND THE *KHANDA*

The symbolism of Ik Oankar in combination with the *khanda* brings together essential elements of the Sikh tradition. Ik Oankar consists of the first two words in the Guru Granth Sahib and means "The Divine Is One." It combines the number "one" and the letter *o*. For Guru Nanak, these two characters together described most completely the essence of Akal Purakh and the monotheistic cornerstone of Sikh belief. Ik Oankar forms the first two words of the Sikh creed

Ik Oankar. Courtesy of sikhchic.com, an online magazine on the art and culture of the Sikh diaspora.

known as the Mul Mantra, the beginning stanza of the first morning hymn sung by Sikhs on a daily basis. *Oankar* is a derivative of the syllable "om" in Vedic traditions, and its central place in Sikh scripture underscores the mystical dimensions of Sikh thought. The term *khanda* is important for Sikhs in that it refers to both the double-edged sword used in the Khalsa initiation ritual and the understanding of divinity as Sarab Loh, or All Steel, since the time of Guru Gobind Singh. It also refers to the primary Sikh emblem of the Khalsa. The *khanda* emblem consists of three parts, a circle, two interlocking sabers, and a double-edged sword in the center. The double-edged sword is encircled by a *chakkar,* a circular blade that represents the oneness of Akal Purakh, without beginning and without end. The two interlocking sabers signify the spiritual and temporal leadership of the Sikh gurus, the sword on the right representing spiritual sovereignty and that on the left, temporal authority. The *khanda* symbol is displayed on the saffron-colored flag that flutters above *gurdwaras* worldwide.

THE FIVE KS

The five symbols worn by initiated Khalsa Sikhs begin with the letter *k*. As mentioned earlier, they are *kesh* (uncut hair), *kangha* (comb), *kachh* (short breeches), *kara* (steel bracelet), and *kirpan* (dagger). Although Sikh tradition maintains that the five *k*s stem from the time Guru Gobind Singh established the Khalsa, their actual origin remains obscure. The earliest texts name only three of these symbols, *kesh, kirpan,* and *kachh,* but make reference to five weapons carried by the early Khalsa Sikhs. The fixed set of five symbols likely came about in the nineteenth century.

There are various meanings attributed to the five *k*s. *Kesh* has been understood as a symbol of holiness and strength. Devout Sikhs believe hair is a gift from God that must be left in its natural state. Wearing the hair uncut also makes Sikhs highly visible as a group. Hair must remain uncut from any part of the body, although many Sikh women pluck their eyebrows and many Sikh men trim their hair and beards while still upholding the basic injunction of keeping their hair long. The *kangha* symbolizes restraint and self-control and is used to keep the uncut hair tidy and in place. This represents both

(Left) *Male Sikh displaying the five ks, Chandigarh, Punjab. Courtesy of Harjant Gill.*

(Below) *Example of small comb* (kangha), *one of the five ks, worn in the hair under the turban. Courtesy of Harjant Gill.*

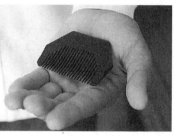

bodily and spiritual purity. The *kangha* also distances Sikhs from other ascetics in India, who often allow their long hair to become matted. *Kachh* represents chastity but was also a useful garment during times of warfare, when warriors needed to get on and off horses quickly. The *kara* is not an ornament but a practical wrist protector on the sword-wielding arm. Without beginning or end, it also stands for the ultimate unity of Akal Purakh. The *kirpan,* often viewed as a ceremonial sword, can be a few inches to three feet long. It represents the Sikh struggle against injustice. Sikhs who are not initiated but still follow the Sikh Reht Maryada often wear some of these symbols, especially the *kara* and the *kirpan.* Some Sikhs wear the *kirpan* as a symbol on a bracelet or necklace.

Sikh Rites of Passage

BIRTH AND NAMING

Sikhs regard children as a gift from God. Upon the birth of a child, some families visit the local *gurdwara* for a special naming ceremony. Others carry out this ritual at home. In some devout Sikh families, the baby is given a taste of nectar made from sugar dissolved in water and stirred with a *kirpan,* which is then carefully placed on the baby's tongue. The baby's mother then drinks the rest of the sanctified water. For many families, however, the ceremony is marked by simple thanksgiving prayers for the child. Then, by randomly opening the Guru Granth Sahib, it is in effect "consulted" as to the baby's name; the first letter of the first word on the left-hand page is used by the parents to choose the baby's name. If the ritual takes place in a *gurdwara,* the name is announced by the *granthi.* Girls' names are followed by the second name Kaur, and boys are given the additional name Singh. After more scripture passages are read, prayers offered, and sweets shared by all, the naming ceremony comes to an end. Many Sikh families, however, simply choose a name with no religious ceremony to mark it.

By and large, Indian family systems, including those of Punjabi Sikhs, are patrilineal. Patriarchal attitudes valuing sons over daughters are the norm, for it is the son who carries on the family name, receives the family inheritance, and, no less important, performs the funeral rites for his parents. For these reasons, the birth of a son is marked by great rejoicing while the birth of a daughter is a much quieter affair. The Indian festival celebrating the birth of sons, Lohri, is also celebrated by Sikhs. Although in some instances the birth of a girl has been included in Lohri celebrations, the festival remains a near-exclusive focus on sons.

MARRIAGE

Following the example of their gurus, Sikhs regard the householder as the ideal and the foundation of society. Guru Nanak and the majority of subsequent gurus married and had children, thus rejecting the Hindu ideal of the celibate ascetic. Sikhs today are expected to marry and have children to continue the family line. They are also required to marry other Sikhs. This is particularly the case for Sikh women.

The engagement ceremony generally takes place in the groom's home, whereas the wedding usually takes place in the bride's town, either at home or in the local *gurdwara.* Two days before the wedding, the bride and groom separately take part in a practice led by their respective mothers, wherein other female relatives rub a special paste of turmeric, flour, and oil onto the hands, arms, and faces of the bride or groom, accompanied by the singing of traditional Punjabi wedding songs. Families then hand out special sweets to those assembled and other friends and relatives. The day before the marriage, another ceremony, known as the bangle ceremony, takes place in the bride's home. Her maternal uncle offers her gifts, including special wedding clothes, and then places ivory-colored bangles on her arms while the women of the family sing traditional wedding songs. The groom is also gifted with special clothes by his maternal uncle. The ceremony is important in recalling the important alliances formed when the mother of the bride or groom entered her new family at the time of her own marriage.

Weddings are generally celebrated in the morning. The marriage ritual begins as normal congregational worship. After the initial morning hymn has been sung, the groom arrives, kneels before the Guru Granth Sahib, and then sits cross-legged facing the sacred scripture. The bride and her attendants follow the same pattern. She then sits to the left of the groom. The *granthi* offers a prayer and seeks the blessings of the Divine. He then gives a brief sermon on the importance of marriage in Sikhism, namely, that marriage is the union of souls similar to the spiritual journey or union of an individual with God.

The bride and groom then make a public statement accepting these ideals by bowing before the Guru Granth Sahib and joining the congregation in prayer. Thereupon the actual marriage ceremony begins, with the bride's father coming forward and symbolically joining the couple by handing the hem of the groom's shoulder scarf to the bride.

The *granthi* then reads the wedding hymn composed by Guru Ram Das. While the *ragis* sing the first verse the groom leads his bride slowly around the Guru Granth Sahib in a clockwise direction. After being seated, the second verse is read, and when the *ragis* begin to sing again, the couple once more circles the scripture. This takes place four times. Upon returning to their place after each circling, the couple kneels before the Guru Granth Sahib. On rare occasions, attempts have been made to make the symbolism between the bride and groom more egalitarian, with the bride taking turns leading the groom. These challenges to tradition have been met with serious opposition, and most Sikh couples are content to stay within the pre-scribed tradition of the groom leading the bride. The service ends with the singing of hymns, followed by the congregational prayer. The congregation is then offered sanctified sweets, which formally concludes the religious portion of the marriage ceremony.

The couple then departs for either for the bride's home or to a marriage hall for a reception. After the reception, the couple leaves for the groom's home, where his extended family is waiting to wel-come its newest member. In keeping with Sikh and Indian tradi-tions, the bride will spend the rest of her life with her husband in his family home. Though in some cases this practice is changing be-cause of a weakening of the extended family system, both in India and in the new homelands, many if not most Sikhs follow the tradi-tional practice.

Divorce, particularly its apparent rise in the Sikh community (as in many others), is fraught with difficulties. For Sikhs, marriage is a spiritual union that must be upheld; the gurus described this union as a single soul residing in two bodies. The Sikh Reht Mary-ada does not even mention divorce. When marriages break down, because Sikhs have no specific code in Indian law, they (along with Buddhists and Jains) are included within the stipulations for divorce in the Hindu Marriage Act of 1955. Sikhs are thus in a legal position to obtain support in the case of divorce. Sikhs in other countries fol-low the marriage and divorce laws in their country of residence.

Divorce is considered dishonorable to both the family system and the community at large, yet, as in other communities, divorce is on the increase among Sikhs. The wife and her family of origin carry the weight of dishonor associated with divorce, in keeping with the pa-triarchal norms of Sikh society. For this reason, many Sikh women stay in their marriages at all costs. While the prevailing notions of honor generally restrict remarriage possibilities, divorcees are gener-ally in a similar situation as widows, who may remarry.

Homosexual behavior is also not condoned in Sikhism, although the Adi Granth and Sikh Reht Maryada are silent on this issue. In rare instances, gay or lesbian Sikh activists have interpreted this omission as allowing for the possibility of same-sex unions. However, given the householder ideal, any form of family or sexual relations that is not procreative and within the bounds of marriage is opposed. Most Sikhs would interpret this as pertaining to homosexual unions.

DEATH RITUALS

Death, like birth and marriage, is regarded as having a spiritual dimension. Similar to Hinduism, in Sikhism, transmigration of the soul is understood as a movement into another state and depends on one's karma. Sikh doctrine stresses that death represents a transition from a life filled with worldly cares to the possibility of a joyous and ultimate union with divinity. Sikh funeral rituals focus on this hope for spiritual fulfillment and also stress that in death as in life, all must submit to the loving will of Akal Purakh.

Sikhs, as in the majority of other Indian religions, practice cremation, which generally takes place on the day of the death of the loved one. For residents outside India, cremation takes place as soon as possible after death. According to the Sikh Reht Maryada, after the body has been ritually cleaned and clothed by close family members, it is adorned with the five *k*s as well as a turban if the deceased is male. Like most important ritual events, though immediately focused on the family, death rituals are public events. In procession, mourners slowly follow the eldest son and male relatives carrying the wooden frame or bier to the cremation grounds outside town. As they walk, the mourners sing specific hymns from the Guru Granth Sahib. According to Sikh tradition, women in the family may not take part in carrying the bier or in lighting the funeral pyre. They are prohibited from even entering the cremation grounds.

Once male members of the family and friends have arrived at the cremation grounds, the *granthi* recites a prayer specific to the death ritual, and then a ritual lighting of the funeral pyre is carried out by the closest male relation, ideally by the eldest son. During this time, those assembled continue to sing appropriate hymns. Prayers end the ceremony, upon which the mourners return to the home of the deceased or to the *gurdwara* for a meal. A continuous reading for forty-eight hours of the Guru Granth Sahib then begins, although in many families the reading is done intermittently over a period of ten days. In India, the ashes are collected within a few days of the cremation and scattered in a chosen river.

TURBAN-TYING CEREMONY

The turban is an essential aspect of Sikh identity, though it is not among the five *k*s. The length of a turban varies from five to six yards, and in families where males generally wear turbans a special turban-tying ceremony may take place. There is no specific age prescribed, although the ceremony often takes place during youth. Families meet either in the *gurdwara* or at home but always in the presence of the Guru Granth Sahib, before which prayers are said accompanied by particular hymns. Parents and friends then give gifts to the young man. Traditionally, there is no similar rite of passage for girls. However, a recent development among a minority of diaspora Sikhs involves young women also choosing to wear a turban. In India the practice is virtually nonexistent. Sikh women instead cover their heads with a light scarf whenever they enter a *gurdwara* or even when they are in the presence of elder male family members.

KHALSA INITIATION: *AMRIT SANSKAR*
AND *KHANDE DI PAHUL*

At the center of the Khalsa initiation order, the *amrit sanskar (amrit,* "nectar of immortality," *sanskar,* "life-cycle rite"), is the sword ritual *(khande di pahul).* The ritual is open to both men and women who lead lives of devotion and believe in the ideals of the Khalsa. The earliest versions of Sikh codes of conduct did not allow women to participate in this rite. The reforms by the Singh Sabha movement made important changes in this regard, and women have since the early twentieth century been allowed to take part in this initiation ritual. While there are no age limits placed on participation, the initiate must be old enough to understand the implications of becoming part of the Khalsa order.

Before the ritual, each participant must bathe, wash his or her hair, remove all jewelry, and wear the five *k*s. The initiation takes place before an open copy of the Guru Granth Sahib and must be accompanied by five initiated Sikhs. These five are the officiants who administer the sacred rite. While any initiated Sikh in good standing can officiate, because the original five beloved ones were male, females are traditionally excluded from acting as officiants. Moreover, the five must be physically whole and free from chronic diseases, as well as necessarily leading exemplary lives. Though these traditions and injunctions may be perceived as discriminatory against women and disabled Sikhs, the masculine warrior ideal generally continues to supersede the ideal of egalitarianism in the Sikh community.

The initiate stands before the Guru Granth Sahib with palms joined in reverence. One of the five officiants gives a short introduction on the meaning of the Khalsa initiation, says a prayer, then opens the scripture at random for a reading. The officiants pour fresh water and sugar crystals into a large iron bowl, thus preparing the sanctified nectar to be used in the initiation ritual. The five kneel around the bowl. Four place both hands on the bowl while one recites specific passages from the Guru Granth Sahib while placing his left hand on the rim of the bowl and using his right to stir the nectar with a double-edged sword. After the reading, the candidate is invited to kneel before the iron bowl and cup his or her hands, into which a handful of nectar is poured and then consumed. This is repeated four times. After each drink the officiant calls out the Khalsa salutation *Vahiguruji ka Khalsa, Vahiguruji ki fateh,* which is then repeated by the initiate. The greeting is followed by the officiant's touching the initiate's eyes with the sweetened water five times, the same greeting called and repeated, and last, the nectar is sprinkled on the hair of the initiate. This is followed by the call and response of the greeting. Any remaining sweetened water is drunk by the initiate. In unison, the five then state the Sikh creed, the Mul Mantra, which is then repeated by the initiate. Injunctions from the Sikh Reht Maryada are expounded and prayers are said, followed by a randomly selected reading from the Guru Granth Sahib. If the initiate was not named at birth with a name chosen from the Guru Granth Sahib, she or he will be renamed. Any name must include Singh for men and Kaur for women. The ceremony concludes with a distribution of sanctified sweets to the initiate.

This ritual abounds with symbols of equality for Sikhs. In the sharing of the nectar and the partaking of sweets from one vessel, the egalitarian ideals from Guru Nanak through to the time of Guru Gobind Singh are clearly demonstrated. New members of the Khalsa order are expected to fully accept and follow these injunctions.

Sikh Identity

While stressing the importance of the Khalsa ideal, the definition of a Sikh, according to the Sikh Reht Maryada, attempts to be inclusive. It states that anyone who has faith in one God, in the ten gurus and their teachings, and in the primacy of the Guru Granth Sahib, and does not adhere to any other religion is a Sikh. It does continue with the statement that a Sikh is one who believes in the necessity and importance of initiation into the Khalsa order. While attempts have been made to limit the definition of a Sikh to one who is committed to wearing the five *k*s, the definition from the Sikh Reht Maryada from 1950 continues to prevail.

Although the majority of Sikhs are not formally initiated members of the Khalsa order, those who are initiated are *amritdhari* Sikhs, Sikhs who have undergone the initiation ritual. This rite holds a special place in the Sikh religion, and the status of the *amritdhari* is perceived as the ideal to which many Sikhs aspire. Many Sikhs are instead *keshdharis,* literally, those with uncut hair. *Keshdharis* follow some if not all the injunctions of the tenth guru in terms of the code of Sikh discipline, including the five *k*s, but are not formally initiated into the order. Sikhs who do not wear all the five *k*s and who cut their hair are often identified as *sahajdhari* Sikhs. *Sahajdhari* has come to mean a Sikh who is a "slow adopter," one who is in the process of becoming a Khalsa Sikh but has not yet attained the necessary spiritual development to undergo the initiation. The notion of "slow adopter" is actually misleading since many Sikhs who cut their hair have no intention of becoming part of the Khalsa order, despite being devoted Sikhs. A Sikh who has undergone initiation but has subsequently cut her or his hair or is not following all the injunctions of the Sikh Reht Maryada is known as an apostate. Once identified as an apostate, however, one may make a public confession of wrongdoing, be assigned a penance, and then reinitiated into the order. Many Sikh families include members who are Khalsa and others who are not.

There have been various times in the history of Sikhism since the establishment of the Khalsa order by Guru Gobind Singh that Sikhs were more likely to follow their guru's call regarding initiation. The period of British rule in India was one such time. Sikhs were highly valued in the British Army, but in order to join the army, British officials insisted that all Sikhs had to undergo initiation into the Khalsa order. It was believed that Sikhs would be better soldiers if they adhered to the martial symbolism of the Khalsa.

Sikh identity has come to the fore especially during times when the Sikh community felt threatened. As noted, the years surrounding 1984 were highly important in terms of reevaluating Sikh identity. Sant Jarnail Singh Bhindranwale insisted that Sikhs reject all identities except the *amritdhari* one. The issue of Sikh identity has reemerged most recently since the tragic events of 9/11, particularly among American Khalsa Sikhs since they have repeatedly been mistaken for followers of the turbaned Osama bin Laden.

Martyrdom

The concept of martyrdom with its Islamic roots in the notion of death "giving witness" to a righteous cause has become an important institution for Sikhs. As the gurus gained increasing political power in their spiritual domains, they began to draw the ire of the authorities around them. According to Sikh tradition, Guru Arjan, the first martyr, was burned alive by his captors. Guru Hargobind took up arms because of his father's death at the hands of the Moguls. Sikh accounts maintain that the ninth master, Guru Tegh Bahadur, was beheaded as a result of his intercession for the religious rights of a group of Brahmins who were being coerced into conversion to Islam. His death is understood as a significant factor in the creation of the militaristic Khalsa order by his son, Guru Gobind Singh, who believed Sikhs should not only fight for the sake of righteousness but also be recognizable as Sikhs in the defense of righteousness.

After the death of Guru Gobind Singh's sons, two of whom are believed to have been immured for refusing to convert to Islam, the concept of dying for a righteous cause took on added significance, and this increased during Banda Bahadur's leadership of the Sikhs. Authorized by Guru Gobind Singh to punish those who persecuted Sikhs, Banda Bahadur rallied a mainly peasant army to avenge attacks against the Sikhs, especially at sites where the cruelest atrocities had taken place. He too was eventually captured, tortured, and put to death by the Moguls, and he is esteemed today as a martyr of the highest order.

More blood flowed during the eighteenth century at the arrival of a new foe, Afghan invaders from the north. Since the Sikhs were vastly outnumbered by the Afghans, their defense had in the main the character of guerrilla warfare. These times of warfare are understood by Sikhs as resistance to oppression; they are often described as a Sikh holocaust.

Those who died are revered as having offered the supreme sacrifice for the cause of righteousness. One Sikh warrior, Baba Dip Singh, who is believed to have had miraculous powers, is written of as having continued fighting even after receiving a fatal blow from his Afghan assailant. Pictures celebrating his martyrdom show him fighting with a sword in one hand and his own severed head in the other.

Although the term "martyr" was not used before the nineteenth century, martyrdom has become an established institution in Sikhism through the retelling of these and other heroic events. It is perceived as an ideal to inspire piety and bravery in Sikhs.

As noted, the 1980s were a time of political instability in Punjab. Sant Jarnail Singh Bhindranwale is seen by many Sikhs today as a modern martyr. Martyrdom continues to hold a fascination and even reverence of many Sikhs. Some *gurdwaras* display particularly graphic pictures of instances of Sikh martyrdom.

Authority in Sikhism

The question of authority in Sikhism is an important one because there is not one organizational hierarchy that applies to all Sikhs living in all parts of the world. It is best to understand Sikhism as having various layers of authority embedded within it. Above all, however, the Guru Granth Sahib is for the vast majority of Sikhs the "text as guru" and the living word of ultimate authority. One manifestation of this authority is a divine order *(hukam)* in the form of a passage from the Guru Granth Sahib chosen at random to guide the daily activities of Sikhs. In the age of the Internet, a divine order from Harimandir Sahib can be accessed immediately by Sikhs around the world.

In addition to spiritual authority are temporal sources of authority, the most important being the Akal Takht, adjacent to Harimandir Sahib in Amritsar and established by Guru Hargobind. There
are four additional authoritative centers revered by Sikhs in various
parts of Punjab and India. These centers are associated with important events in the life of Guru Gobind Singh. Each is led by a male
Sikh regarded as authoritative as the chief officiate of that particular
center. Diversity among them exists with regard to what constitutes
"scripture." Whereas the Guru Granth Sahib is generally understood
as the sole scriptural authority, a number of centers grant both it and
the Dasam Granth scriptural authority.

The Shiromani Gurdwara Parbandhak Committee (SGPC) is
another important Sikh institution. It is headed by an elected administration that is in charge of maintaining the *gurdwaras* in Punjab. While historically having a central role, the SGPC's authority
does not actually extend far beyond Punjab's *gurdwaras* and shrines.
Other administrative bodies have consequently formed in other
parts of India and overseas in an attempt to manage regional *gurdwaras*. Most of have failed, however, to exercise legal sway over more
than a few *gurdwaras*.

Perhaps more than any other locus of authority, the local congregation tends to play the most important part in terms of the everyday workings of the Sikh community. In most cases, each congregation acts entirely autonomously, with elected officials maintaining
the affairs of each *gurdwara*. This independent authority is particularly important in overseas Sikh communities, where the central
Punjab institutions have less reach and influence. The *granthis,* who
are hired by the congregation as the official caretakers of the *gurdwara* and often as readers of the Guru Granth Sahib, do not generally
have special authority or leadership functions.

Another form of authority in Sikhism today resides in those considered saints, called sants. These are men (almost exclusively) who
have a devoted following because of their piety or even their perceived
supernatural powers. These sants are not to be confused with living
guru lineages, although the line separating them is at times difficult to ascertain. A Sikh sant can exert a great deal of authority over
the lives of his followers, both in India and in overseas communities.

In some cases, these authoritative figures have become leaders of alternative Sikh groups with their own *gurdwaras*. These *gurdwaras* differ from traditional ones in not having elected committees running the affairs of the *gurdwara*. Important decisions are instead made by the sant. This authority often extends to immediate and personal matters facing their adherents.

Because some of these individuals may support beliefs and practices that differ from those of mainstream Sikhs, some Sikhs view these figures with suspicion. This is particularly the case given the clear rejection of living guruship in mainstream Sikhism; attitudes resembling devotion or reverence toward another human being or indications of the immense power held by many of these individuals cause severe discomfort to many Sikhs. Nonetheless, certain individuals continue to hold sway over large numbers of their Sikh devotees, in India and in the Sikh diaspora.

CHAPTER 4

Sikh Society

Visitors to Punjab are often amazed at the warmth and openness of its people. My family and I have been welcomed into strangers' homes and enjoyed hearty meals cooked on the spot for us on countless occasions. The work ethic that Punjabis take great pride in is apparent as one drives through the thriving farmlands and bustling cities. Through conversation and observation, one also becomes aware of the traditional and largely patriarchal values and practices holding sway in present-day Sikh families, whether in India or in the vast Sikh diaspora. While there is much of Punjabi Sikh society to explore, this chapter focuses on gender, kinship and marriage patterns, caste, and alternative religious practices of the Sikhs.

Sikhism and Gender

The Sikh tradition offers a fascinating window into what appear to be vastly divergent attitudes and practices with regard to gender. One of the highest positions of authority for Sikhs was held, in both 1999 and 2004, by Bibi Jagir Kaur, the first female president of the Shiromani Gurdwara Parbandhak Committee (SGPC). (Though heralded as a great achievement for Sikh women's rights, Jagir Kaur's tenure was clouded by controversy, including criminal charges, eventually forcing her from the presidency.) Despite a Sikh woman's having held an important position in the religious and political organization of Punjab, Sikh women are barred from participating in certain rituals at the most sacred of Sikh shrines, Harimandir Sahib, simply because of their gender. Punjab's Sikhs also hold the dubious distinction of having some of the lowest female birthrates in all of India. Moreover, whereas Sikh religious tenets offer women the possibility of complete liberation, it is difficult to find more than mere mention of women throughout Sikh history.

The centrality of the householder ideal espoused by Guru Nanak is helpful in understanding the place of women in the early Sikh community. By rejecting the ascetic route to liberation in favor of that of the householder, Guru Nanak clearly provided a path to liberation to women as well as men. Akal Purakh was accessible to all, especially within family and social systems. The Divine could be found within the everyday workings of society. By the gurus' insistence on the primacy of the fellowship of believers, both women and men were provided a community in which through service, devotion, and love they could transform their lives. The gurus also used female imagery in their hymns and characterized Akal Purakh as beyond gender limitations.

Guru Amar Das criticized the custom of widow burning, and there is evidence the guru challenged women's obligation to wear a veil in public. Nonetheless, although Sikhs proclaim that Sikhism is inherently egalitarian, the issue is more complex. While the gurus insisted that neither caste nor gender were barriers to spiritual liberation, such issues were addressed within long-established, patriarchal social structures that were in place. The hymns speak of ideal womanhood in the context of family life, filling the roles of good sister, daughter, wife, and mother. Norms of modesty and honor were to be upheld by both women and men; many hymns clearly disapprove of behavior outside accepted social and sexual standards.

Sikh history is generally silent about the actual roles of women in the development of Sikhism. The Adi Granth mentions the name of only one of the gurus' wives, Mata Khivi, Guru Angad's wife, who is recalled as supervising the communal kitchen and caring for pilgrims traveling to the center Khadur. The *janamsakhis* fill the void with details of the wives and children of the gurus, although they contain inconsistencies, especially with regard to the naming of gurus' daughters and even the wives of the gurus. Guru Nanak's sister, Nanaki, is portrayed as fully supportive of her brother during the early development of the Sikh community. Bibi Amro, the daughter of the second guru, Angad, is remembered as the one who initially drew Guru Amar Das into the community by her beautiful singing of the guru's compositions. Bibi Bhani, the daughter of the third guru and wife of the fourth, is in some sources credited with influencing the changes effected in the pattern of guru succession. There are also indications of women helping with established congregations and preaching the message of the early gurus during the time of the community's development. With the institutionalization of deputies and greater complexity of Sikh organization, women took on less-central roles.

There is no indication that women were invited to join the Khalsa order, nor were they to be initiated through the sword ritual inaugurated by Guru Gobind Singh. Also, despite the popular conception of women receiving the name Kaur during this time, historical evidence points only to males being given an honorary name, Singh, associated with the order. This is not difficult to understand in light of the tenth guru's call to take up arms to create a military order. The adopted symbolism of the Khalsa order was overtly military. Evidence suggests that those not initiated into the Khalsa order came to be viewed as a lesser order of Sikhs. Significantly, however, Mata Sundri, one of the three wives of Guru Gobind Singh, upon her husband's death, occupied an important leadership role during one of the most tumultuous times in the community's history. Mata Sundri led the community longer than any of the nine gurus subsequent to Guru Nanak, though there is surprisingly little said of her in Sikh historical accounts. Another wife of the guru, Mata Sahib Devan, is designated as the Mother of the Khalsa, thus honored with her husband, Guru Gobind Singh.

The role of women in the Sikh tradition was an important focus of the Singh Sabha reformers in the nineteenth and early twentieth centuries given that Sikh identity had, since the time of Guru Gobind Singh, focused on Sikh males. Reformers felt the need for identity markers for Sikh women to distinguish them from women of other religious communities. One marker among the upper classes that differentiated Hindu and Muslim women was naming practices. Whereas women were generally known by only one name, in some cases Hindu women added the name Devan or Devi (goddess), and

Muslim women of the upper ranks of society often bore Begum as an additional name. Sikh women were also called Devi if they had more than one name.

For the purpose of distinguishing Sikh women from their Muslim and Hindu counterparts, reformers turned to an obscure tradition. The Rajput name Singh had been associated with Sikhs since the time of Guru Gobind Singh's establishment of the Khalsa order. Kshatriya Rajputs, who bore the name Singh, were famous for their military traditions. Other Rajput names included Kanwar (prince), and its Punjabi version was Kaur, used among certain sectors in Sikh society for both males and females. Kaur eventually came to be associated with Sikh females, where it meant "princess." Given its association with royalty, most women named Kaur were of the Jat Sikh aristocracy stemming from the confederacy period.

Reformers saw in this political and cultural signifier an important means for distinguishing Sikh women from their coreligionists, and a rather obscure cultural tradition was thus legitimized with religious significance. It is important to note that Sikh history was rewritten to give this naming practice deep historical roots. Related to this, a number of the gurus' wives have subsequently been renamed. Sahib Devan, one of Guru Gobind Singh's wives, is reidentified as Sahib Kaur in the texts written by the Singh Sabha reformers.

Moreover, while the earliest texts are either silent about women's roles in initiation practices or reject women's initiation into the Khalsa order, Singh Sabha reformers perceived a need to establish a truly egalitarian tradition and so sought to make changes. They viewed the lack of women as part of the prescribed Khalsa identity as problematic to their wider goals of Sikh reform. When women were initiated into the Khalsa order in the late nineteenth and early twentieth centuries, female initiation was distinguished from its male counterpart through the use of a single-edged sword instead of the double-edged sword prescribed by Guru Gobind Singh. Eventually, however, both women and men underwent initiation by the double-edged sword associated with the order, a tradition that continues today.

All these changes took place amid much conflict among Sikh groups. Whereas educated reformers believed that their purifying efforts were essential to the well-being of the Sikh tradition, the bulk of the Sikh populace was little affected by the concerns of the educated elite. However, over time, the reformers' efforts bore fruit, especially with regard to incorporating the name Kaur for women, though this too was a long process. In the codes of conduct laid down in the early twentieth century, initiated women were given the name Kaur. With the finalization of the official Sikh Reht Maryada in 1950, the Sikh naming practice shifted once again. It stipulated that Kaur was to be given to all Sikh girls and Singh to all Sikh boys at the time of birth, a practice followed by Sikhs today.

Despite some of the egalitarian principles introduced by the Sikh gurus, discriminatory attitudes in the Sikh community toward women continue. Female infanticide, though condemned by the gurus, continued to be widely practiced in Sikh society. Today, technology has provided a new way to determine the sex of a fetus and abort unwanted females, an occurrence happening particularly among Sikhs in Punjab, who constitute the majority of the population. This appears to be a growing trend in Punjabi society, inasmuch as according to the 2001 census, the child sex ratio in Punjab was 793 girls per 1,000 boys, in comparison with the ratio of 894 to 1,000 in 1961. Although laws have been passed in an attempt to stop the abuse, the abortion of female fetuses continues at an alarming rate among Sikhs.

Some discriminatory attitudes associated with ancient Indian views of women's impurity and menstrual pollution persist, despite the gurus' exhorting their followers not to perceive anything in God's creation as having the inherent ability to pollute. This and similar attitudes are being challenged by Sikhs, who have been raised to believe that the Sikh religion is unparalleled in terms of its egalitarian principles. For example, there have been instances of Sikh women, especially from the diaspora communities, challenging what they perceive as discriminatory practices at Harimandir Sahib. They have targeted the fact that no women serve as *ragis* in the shrine. Recently, a number of Sikh women from the diaspora were prohibited from taking part in an important ritual procession at Harimandir Sahib. An extensive grassroots protest was launched, insisting on women's equal rights in all facets of ritual and devotional life at this most holy and revered shrine. Although these protests have not resulted in actual changes, they have been important consciousness-raising initiatives that have reverberated throughout the worldwide Sikh community and have caused Sikhs to reevaluate the position of women in their tradition. Sikh women have also begun to challenge the tradition of only males participating as the five beloved ones.

Sikh women thus face hurdles similar to those of their counterparts in other male-dominated religious traditions. Sikh women take solace from the doctrinal support they claim from various sources, including scripture, the examples of eminent Sikh women of history, as well as the egalitarian practices promoted by the Sikh Reht Maryada, as they continue to challenge deeply ingrained patriarchal values and practices in their tradition.

Family Honor

Many of the expectations related to family values in Punjab are unwritten codes and reflect customary values. Central to this value system are kinship rules shared by Sikhs and those of other religious traditions. Kinship roles are understood throughout South Asia as essentially unchanging and as the basis of social organization. Women's identities and status are ultimately linked to their roles as daughters, daughters-in-law, mothers, and wives. Abiding by these relational norms ensures family position and honor are maintained; dishonorable conduct, on the other hand, can lead to the damaging of family honor. Daughters in particular are continually made aware that if they behave dishonorably, they will bring deep shame to their family.

Gender inequity and women's subordination are firmly fixed in societal structures, kinship, and marriage practices. Closely associated with the notion of honor *(izzat)*, especially for women, is modesty and propriety *(sharam)*. For Punjabi males, honor is attained through wealth, status, and individual actions, but also through the behavior of in particular their wives, daughters, and sisters. Honor and propriety together occupy an important role in maintaining the traditional patriarchal framework of Punjabi society. Loss of honor and propriety has traditionally pertained especially to women's behavior. An individual's loss of honor is no less than a loss of family honor and in turn a decline in a family's social standing. For these reasons, kinship rules surrounding female behavior are more stringently enforced than those for males.

Marriage Practices

Although "love marriages" are not unknown in India, the vast majority of Sikh marriages are arranged by the parents or kin of the couple. This is the case in the Indian context and in the Sikh diaspora. Such marriages forge important family alliances; parents believe their experience, contacts, maturity, and judgment make them best suited for arranging such unions and ensuring their success. The family unit is evaluated on two levels: how well children fulfill their parents' expectations, particularly with regard to traditional values, including marriage and abiding by their religious injunctions, and, second, how the community views the family.

Marriage, regardless of religious, class, caste, or regional differences, is the pivotal event in an individual's life, for with it comes a thorough transformation of identity, role, and status. For women, this includes a change in residence as well. Sikh marriages generally follow rules of hypergamy, namely, the bride and her family are considered to have a lower social status than the groom and his family. This traditional hierarchy is followed by families throughout the different religious communities in India, including Sikhs. This is based on the notion of the "gift of the virgin" and the deference due to the groom and his family upon acceptance of this gift. In Punjab, as in most of India, this gift is accompanied by a dowry. While a woman's dowry was once understood as a replacement for her share of the family inheritance, today it is increasingly viewed as a necessary gift to her husband and his family. In some cases, it is used as an enticement for a potential spouse. This has resulted at times in extortion of the bride's family by her groom or his family.

Upon marriage, a woman is transferred from her father's lineage to that of her husband. Her husband and his relatives are then responsible for her care. Marriage is thus a family event since it involves not two individuals but two families in a far-reaching arrangement. Critical to a successful joining of families, on the part of women in particular, continues to be keeping the family name untarnished. Women are thus obliged to exercise propriety before as well as after marriage.

For these reasons, the ending of a marriage is traumatic, whether through divorce or the death of a spouse. To ensure the long life of her husband, a woman is expected to perform ritual fasting. Widowhood is dreaded, not only because of the emotional and often economic deprivation but also because of the guilt and blame heaped on the woman for her lack of devotion. As a member of her husband's family, a widow must ensure her actions not only protect the family from disgrace but also uphold the memory and honor of the deceased.

Although the Sikh Reht Maryada supports widow remarriage, cultural norms belie this provision. Negative attitudes and biases are evident in such Punjabi terms as "discarded" when referring to a divorced woman; "without a husband" and "widow" are common words of abuse. Widows are monitored closely by their husbands' family members to ensure that no dishonor is brought upon the family name. Not surprisingly in this patriarchal hierarchy, the situation is radically different for widowers, who commonly remarry.

LEVIRATE MARRIAGE IN PUNJAB

One form of widow remarriage that was a part of the Punjabi kinship system, particularly among the traditionally agricultural Jat Sikhs, is levirate remarriage. Though rarely practiced today, levirate remarriage historically served as a means to control land within the patrilineal family unit. To ensure the deceased husband's family kept control of its land, a younger brother-in-law or another sibling would take the widow as his wife, even if he was already married. Thus, although monogamy is the norm, polygamous unions also took place in the Sikh community.

The matter of polygamy versus monogamy among the Sikhs is not straightforward given that two Sikh gurus had more than one wife, and although monogamy is considered the norm, the Sikh Reht Maryada does not prohibit polygamy.

Gender and Procreation

Within Punjabi kinship patterns, procreation is understood in the imagery of the land, a defining feature of the primarily rural populace. In this construct, the female provides the field and the male gives the seed. The man's role in procreation is understood as the gift of conception. Similar to property rights and family money, the child of this union is seen as part of the property of the male head of the family. If the child is male, he is then an indivisible part of the patrilineal kinship group. While a girl also receives love and affection from her family, it is also understood that her true home will be that of her future husband's.

The male-dominated family system continues today as the mainstay of Sikh society, held in place largely by various fixed mechanisms of obedience and respect. The depth of devotion required to be considered "a good wife" defines Indian expectations of marriage, expectations tied to deeply religious values that extend beyond any one religious tradition.

From an early age, girls are socialized to the religious and social ideal of being a dutiful and caring wife. Thus, in Sikh culture, though not tied to any specific Sikh tenet, many unmarried Sikh women participate in ritual fasting, as with their Hindu and Muslim counterparts, in order to secure a good husband; once married, the act is intended to ensure a long life, prosperity, and the well-being of the husband. This ritual fasting, according to which a woman abstains from eating or drinking until moonrise, is viewed as a *religious* act inasmuch as one is fulfilling one's duty as a wife and furthering and sustaining the moral order. This ritual act embodies women's status as derived from her husband and also nonexistent without him. This and other acts of devotion contribute to a husband's long life and at the same time to the stability of marriage.

Although change is under way, there are also traditional attitudes endorsing public roles for men while upholding the virtue of domesticity for women. When women do assume public roles, male accompaniment is considered a necessary component.

Sikhism and Caste

The Sikh gurus explicitly rejected caste as an impediment to liberation, insisting in their hymns that emancipation was open to all. The Khalsa initiation rite and the community kitchen confirm this rejection. Yet caste is firmly retained in the Sikh social order and conventions, something the gurus seemed to sanction; the nine gurus who married did so within their Khatri caste and also married their children in accordance with caste norms, thus following traditional Indian marriage customs. The Sikh gurus thus opposed the spiritual ramifications of caste but accepted caste as a form of social organization fundamental to the society in which they lived.

In Punjab as well as in India generally, the rules and customs associated with each caste, of which there are many, allow each individual, family, or group to be situated in the caste hierarchy. How the caste hierarchy is arranged may vary from state to state or region to region. For the majority of Sikhs today, each individual is a member of a larger joint family unit and and of larger caste and subcaste groupings. Many Sikhs take on the name of their subcaste. As noted, most Sikhs today marry within their caste but outside their parents' descent groups. One of the reasons for marrying outside of one's village community relates to prior kinship ties in one's natal village; another is tied to rules of inheritance, which, for the mainly agrarian Sikh population, is connected with land ownership. Marrying outside the kinship group precludes the possibility ancestral land will be subdivided.

Although in the larger Indian caste hierarchy Jats are classified as a low, peasant caste, Jats form the dominant group, in both numbers and power, in Sikh society. Most Jats live in rural areas and make up about 60 percent of the Sikh population. Given the dominance of rural Sikhs and Jat predominance as landowners in Punjab, a sense of Jat superiority over landless castes has existed historically and continues today.

Nonetheless, the Khatri caste, the lineage of the Sikh gurus, though relatively small in numbers occupies an important place in Sikh society, particularly in urban areas. The Ramgarhia caste, whose members were historically carpenters and blacksmiths, forms the next largest group and thus claims some importance in the wider Sikh population. There are also Sikhs who fall within the larger classification known as untouchables, or Dalits, those considered lacking the minimum requirement for fitting within the caste system. Such Sikhs are the Mazhabis and Ravidasis. Dalits of all religious affiliations experience the worst prejudices associated with the caste system and in some cases are not even welcome to enter traditional centers of worship, including Sikh *gurdwaras*. Mazhabis are traditionally sweepers and Ravidasis, skinners and tanners, occupations associated with pollution and impurity.

While there are instances of intercaste marriage between members of different castes among Sikhs, proscriptions are followed with regard to intermarriage with members of the untouchables class. This remains the case even if individual members of the Mazhabi and Ravidasi castes have risen in status by virtue of economic advancement.

Sikhs and Other Religious Practices

In addition to the mainstream religious practices, many individuals, especially in rural areas, take part in beliefs and practices that fall outside their religious identity. These common practices have often been dismissed as popular religion, folk traditions, or even pejoratively as superstition. Yet aspects of these practices are integral to the lived realities of many Punjabis, regardless of their religious affiliation. Many of these practices contribute to an understanding of *lived* religion that is far more diverse than the normative religious traditions as they are generally understood. These "alternative" religious practices exist *within* dominant religions and thus demand the acknowledgment that religious identities are not as neat as often presented in textbooks. In northern India, religious practices that are not "purely" Muslim, Hindu, Christian, or Sikh are followed by adherents from a variety of religions. These include the worship of relics and ancestors, the wearing of amulets (with special stones believed to possess spiritual properties), or the placing of certain objects on homes to ward off evil spirits (e.g., blackened pots set on rooftops). Vehicles carrying bunches of chilies on the rear bumper reflect the belief that they protect their occupants from wayward or evil spirits.

Many Sikhs participate in such religious and cultural practices. In some villages in Punjab, Sikh homes may contain images of Hindu gods and goddesses, for example, Shiva or Durga, though their owners insist they are staunch Sikhs. Some Sikhs worship at Sufi shrines that have a reputation for possessing healing powers. Others may make obeisance to spirits or deities associated with rivers and streams, believing that they receive in return protection and plentiful harvests.

These alternative practices do not suggest Sikhs are confused about their primary religious identity but instead point to a religious complexity and diversity that is in many ways a hallmark of rural Punjabi religion. Many of these practices have long been criticized by Sikh authorities as anti-Sikh, most particularly during the time of the Singh Sabha reforms during British rule. Today, advocates of reform continue to attempt to put a stop to many of these practices, but they continue, deeply ingrained in the society at large.

CHAPTER 5

The Sikh Diaspora

This chapter examines the three countries with the largest Sikh communities outside Punjab, the United Kingdom, Canada, and the United States, with emphasis on key landmarks of Sikh migration to each of these host countries. I begin with a brief overview of a number of dominant characteristics of Sikh diasporic communities worldwide.

The term "diaspora" originally denoted the dispersal of Jews worldwide but is now widely used to describe other religious communities outside their homelands. While there is little consensus with regard to actual numbers, it can be safely said that of about 23 million Sikhs, between 1 and 1.5 million live outside India. The Sikh diaspora represents an important component of Indian migration in that Sikhs constitute a disproportionately high percentage of Indian immigrants worldwide. This is striking in light of Sikhs making up less than 2 percent of the total Indian population. A popular saying among Sikhs notes that "each time a Sikh . . . leaves the homeland, it is simply a return to what is most permanent—the journey," underscoring both the pain of separation from the homeland and the sense of adventure that has long characterized the community. Sikhs of the diaspora are often the most readily identifiable segment of any country's minority ethnic population because of their distinctive identity markers, particularly in the case of adhering to the five *k*s. This has forced host countries to confront often uncomfortable issues with regard to public policy toward certain cultural and religious groups.

Punjabi society is characterized by a generally peaceful and easy coexistence with members of other faith traditions and with popular and heterodox practices shared by all faith communities. In other words, the Punjabi village and rural Punjab on the whole have been lessons in social and religious diversity. The situation is similar for Sikhs in the diaspora.

Migration to most countries containing sizable communities of Sikhs occurred in waves. These waves were generally dependent on what are called push and pull factors. Push factors have included economic considerations (e.g., shrinking landholdings and leaving traditional agrarian occupations for employment in the army) as well as political ones, partition, for example, and the political turmoil following the events of 1984. Pull factors can include changes in a host country's policies toward immigration, generally in response to changing labor conditions or an aging workforce, resulting in demands for new immigration.

Punjab was the last province annexed by the British, and British policies in this, their last frontier, were characteristically different from those in other parts of India. The British favored the Sikhs, perceiving them to be among the finest of the Indian martial races, particularly after the Indian Uprising of 1857; Punjabis and Sikhs in particular had shown loyalty countering the uprising. Although constituting less than 2 percent of the Indian population, Sikhs were especially recruited by the British and eventually made up about 20 percent of the Indian Army. The first Sikhs to go abroad were recruited as soldiers as early as 1858, serving in far-flung arenas such as China, Malaysia, the Middle East, Africa, and Europe. Others were employed as police officers in Hong Kong and in other destinations, including Fiji and Thailand. From there, Sikh migrants made their way to countries such as Australia and New Zealand. As indentured laborers in the late nineteenth century, Ramgarhia Sikhs traveled to Uganda and Kenya and made an important contribution to the construction of the national railway systems.

For most Sikhs in the diaspora, Punjab remains their homeland. Sikhs maintain close spiritual ties with their religious home through various means. Many spend considerable time and money in Punjab supporting philanthropic initiatives in their ancestral villages or by building or upgrading *gurdwaras* in their home regions. They also strengthen spiritual ties by inviting renowned *ragis* and religious leaders and preachers from the important Sikh centers in India. For example, a particularly spiritual leader with a sizable following in India may be invited to a particular country and travel from *gurd-wara* to *gurdwara* exhorting fellow Sikhs to a renewed commitment to their faith while receiving funds for his center in India.

Gurdwaras worldwide occupy an important role beyond that of a center of communal worship. They also serve as schools for Punjabi language and religious classes and as meeting places for elderly Sikhs or women's and youth groups. Some *gurdwaras* have gymnasiums for sports activities. Their function as a language school has become particularly important. Many younger Sikhs cannot speak Punjabi or read the Gurmukhi script and are increasingly opting out of *gurdwara* services. Some *gurdwaras* are attempting to reach their youth by projecting scripture translations onto large screens so they can follow the service.

Another important development in the Sikh diaspora, particularly in countries where many Sikhs reside, is the establishment of independent schools designed to fit the specific needs of Sikh children. These schools, often known as Khalsa schools, are variously funded: from private donations, through a combination of private and public funding available to faith-based schools, or entirely from the state. Although the number of Sikhs attending these schools has remained small, they offer Sikhs a religion-based education with a particular focus on Sikh history and culture, Punjabi language training, and Sikh martial arts while also following each country's curriculum guidelines. Classes may be taught by Sikh or non-Sikh teachers.

Another initiative in the Sikh diaspora is the growing Sikh camp movement, for children, youth, and women, often sponsored by Sikh congregations or by groups not tied to a specific congregation. These are often referred to as *gurmat* camps, *gurmat* meaning "teachings of the gurus." While many of these camps are locally based, a number invite attendees from across the globe. The camps usually operate during the summer months and focus on Sikh scripture, religion, history, and the Punjabi language, simultaneously giving children or youth the opportunity to interact with other young Sikhs. Campers are given the opportunity to discuss issues relevant to their particular age group or circumstances that may not be readily discussed in the *gurdwaras*.

Sikhs also participate in host-country politics, while following closely developments in Punjab. For many Sikhs, a sense of civic responsibility corresponds to deeply held Sikh spiritual aspirations and ideals. From the time of Guru Hargobind's symbolic pairing of the swords of temporal and spiritual authority, Sikhs understand religion and politics as essentially inseparable.

Caste distinctions continue to inform social hierarchies in the Sikh diasporic community, although outward manifestations of caste differences and notions of defilement appear to have greatly diminished. Nonetheless, Sikhs from the most disadvantaged of caste groupings, including the Mazhabis, Bhattras, Ravidasis, and even the Ramgarhias, often distance themselves from *gurdwaras* of higher-caste groups and establish their own caste-based places of worship. This is particularly the case where large Jat Sikh populations exist. Caste is sustained by means of endogamous marriage practices.

Beyond caste divisions, Sikh diaspora communities, as with traditional Punjabi village politics, are often organized around community factions. These factions, generally having little to do with caste or ideology though no less characterized by conflict, are often organized around a leader and loyalty to that leader. Notions of honor, power, and reputation figure significantly in the factions, which appear to be endemic to many Sikh organizations, political, social, economic, religious, or cultural. Factionalism and its associated conflicts often characterize relations between groups in the Sikh diaspora.

Marriage and Kinship Patterns

As in India, family and kinship patterns characterize Sikh society throughout the diaspora. Albeit changes are occurring in traditional family patterns in India, they are being challenged especially among immigrant groups outside the homeland. Many Sikhs live and work in a largely self-contained Punjabi Sikh society (often connected to a local *gurdwara*) that operates within the bounds of traditional Sikh and Punjabi value systems. For many Sikhs, notions of family honor, prestige, and status continue to exert their influences. Most Sikhs place importance on ensuring that one's actions are beyond reproach or shame for the good name of one's family, kinship, and caste group.

Arranged marriages, or assisted or guided marriages as they are sometimes called today, are still the norm for Sikh families worldwide. The reputation of a prospective partner is examined via the closely knit extensive international Sikh network. It is a mere matter of pressing a button in these days of the Internet to investigate the caste, economic status, and other characteristics of a potential bride or groom and their families.

Historically, the bride and even the groom had little to say with regard to a proposed union. In some cases the couple would not even have met before the wedding. The couple could meet before their wedding day only under close supervision. A great deal has changed in this regard. Though families are still heavily involved in their children's marital choices, suggestions and preferences of the prospective bride and groom also figure in the search for a suitable marriage partner.

Some Sikh families turn to their homeland to find a suitable mate for their children, especially for their sons. Young Sikh women from India are often perceived as less tainted by Western social norms and better able to ensure that Sikh family honor is upheld in the host country. In cases where diaspora families turn to large urban centers in India to find mates for their children from similar economic, educational, and social backgrounds, the possibility for a successful union is relatively high. When the differences in life experiences between the bride and groom are significant, however, the strain is at times too great and leads to unhappy marriages or divorce.

Although dating is strongly discouraged for fear of a potential loss of honor, many Sikh youth do date, often without their parents' knowledge. So-called love marriages are also on the increase in the Sikh community, especially when young people leave their extended families for work elsewhere or postsecondary education and take upon themselves the responsibility of finding a marriage partner.

One important aspect of family life in the Sikh diaspora has to do with the extent that the law in the host country, especially in Western countries, intervenes in family matters. In India, despite laws pertaining to marriage, inheritance, divorce, dowry prohibition, and domestic violence, many traditional customs and practices simply disregard these laws with little state intervention. In many other countries, laws and social norms tend to focus more on individual rights as opposed to parental or family authority and privilege. In some cases, this has led to social or legal challenges in Sikh families, particularly regarding inequalities between men and women or generational differences.

Sikh family patterns are changing in many countries of the Sikh diaspora, especially in the United Kingdom, Canada, and the United States, where the majority of Sikhs live in large cities. This is in marked contrast to Sikhs' mainly rural base in Punjab, where patriarchal traditions related to control of ancestral lands were strong. Though the extended family unit continues to thrive in these host countries, there have been important changes in traditional family hierarchies. Immigration patterns have typically depended on one male member of a family immigrating to a host country, then sponsoring additional male kin. Only once these individuals are fairly well established are wives and families sponsored as well. Indian tradition demands that parents are taken care of by the eldest son, and thus elderly parents often immigrate to a son's host country after their retirement in India. However, in many host countries, these senior family members often fall into a more marginal, even dependent role in contrast with a traditional Punjabi village household, which is built upon the rule of the eldest patriarch.

Another significant difference relates to the new reality of both women and men working outside the home. This has led to great economic success in many diasporic Sikh communities, but it has also led, often in combination with the influence of Western individualist values, to a reevaluation of family roles and authority. For younger Sikhs in particular, this new reality has provoked challenges to the traditional patriarchal power dynamics in Sikh families.

Sikhs and Academia

As Sikhs have become established in various parts of the world, they and their traditions have also gained visibility in institutions of higher learning. Textbooks in world religions thirty years ago rarely included discussion of Sikhism. Today, however, it occupies a respectable place in world religion studies at many Western universities. In North America there are now special programs or chairs of Sikh studies, the University of Toronto becoming the first institution to offer a program in Sikh studies in 1986.

Dr. W. Hew McLeod (1932–2009), of New Zealand, was the most preeminent Western scholar in Sikh studies. Beginning with his *Guru Nanak and the Sikh Religion,* first published in 1968, his work has had a major impact on the study of Sikhism. McLeod applied the critical methodologies standard in Western historical analysis to some of the canonical texts of Sikhism. His questioning of the historical accuracy of some of these texts, including the *janamsakhis,* caused much discomfort in some segments of the Sikh community worldwide. The controversies surrounding Dr. McLeod and later scholars of Sikhism working within similar frameworks is comparable to the battles fought in the nineteenth century (some of which persist) in Jewish and Christian studies, when the historicity of the Jewish scriptures and Christian gospels were questioned. Nonetheless, Sikh studies are flourishing. Publications on different aspects of Sikhism and the Sikhs and courses on Sikhism are increasing. International conferences are raising research in Sikh studies to a new level of sophistication and complexity.

Sikhs and the Arts

One important aspect of the Sikh experience in various parts of the diaspora has been a growing awareness that the preservation and showcasing of Sikh art and culture are vital for raising the Sikh profile in the host country. A primary objective of the Sikh Foundation, based in California, has been the promotion of the heritage of the Sikhs through art and culture, and the results have been impressive. In 1999, the Victoria and Albert Museum put on an exhibition titled The Art of the Sikh Kingdoms, which then traveled to Canada's Royal Ontario Museum in 2000. The Smithsonian's National Museum of Natural History showcased Sikhs: Legacy of the Punjab in 2004. New York's Rubin Museum of Art featured an exhibition entitled I See No Stranger: Early Sikh Art and Devotion in 2006, the first of its kind in that city. The first permanent Sikh collection in North America is housed at the Asian Art Museum of San Francisco. These exhibits, in some of the finest galleries in the world, have led to a significant development of Sikh art and Sikh art collections in the diaspora. These advances have allowed Sikhs to reach out to the wider community in new ways and further an understanding of Sikh identity beyond an exclusively religious focus.

Sikhs in the United Kingdom

Britain contains the largest Sikh community outside India. According to the 2001 census, about three hundred fifty thousand Sikhs reside in the United Kingdom. As in other countries with significant Sikh communities, the actual number of Sikhs there is likely higher than official estimates.

The most famous of the early Sikh migrants was Dalip Singh, a son of Maharajah Ranjit Singh, the great "Lion of Punjab," and one of his numerous wives, Maharani Jind Kaur. Dalip Singh had succeeded his half brother, Sher Singh, to the crown in 1843 and was thus the last ruler of Punjab before being exiled to Britain in 1854 at the age of fifteen after the annexation of Punjab by the British in 1849. Soon thereafter Dalip Singh converted to Christianity. He became a country squire very much at home in the company of British aristocrats. He lived on a pension from the East India Company but fell into debt due to his large family and expensive tastes. Near the end of his life he reconverted to Sikhism and attempted to return to India to take up his rightful place as ruler of Punjab. His plans were thwarted, however, and he died a lonely death in a hotel room in Paris. He is buried at the Elveden Church in Suffolk, beside his wife Maharani Bamba, and one of his sons, Prince Edward Albert Duleep Singh.

SIKH PATTERNS OF MIGRATION TO BRITAIN

From the 1890s to World War I, only a few Sikh visitors, students and soldiers, arrived in Britain. Soldiers especially came for Queen Victoria's Golden Jubilee in 1887 and later for the coronation of King Edward VII in 1902.

During the interwar years, the first number of Sikh migrants arrived to settle in Britain, likely with a small number of Muslims from certain villages with relatives and other associates in Britain, including a small number of Sikhs. Britain's rapid industrial growth following World War II created a demand for labor. Former colonies were sources of cheap labor, and British policies changed to allow for a significant influx of migrants to meet this demand. Sikh settlers worked in foundries, in textile factories, and at similar industrial sites usually in inner cities, most seeing themselves as temporary residents working to raise enough capital to return to Punjab and rebuild their lives in their homeland. For most, however, the low-paying jobs open to them led instead to what has been called the myth of return, an experience common to most South Asian migrants. The myth has had a pivotal organizational and attitudinal effect, causing many migrants to perceive their settlement as temporary and thus maintain a strong Sikh identity within Britain and show little interest in integrating into the wider British society.

Mass migration to Britain began as a result of the partition, with many dislocated Sikhs risking all for a new start in Britain. In 1968 the British government passed the Commonwealth Immigration Act, an attempt to deal more effectively with discrimination and other disadvantages suffered by recent immigrants by providing housing, expanded employment, and other opportunities. These improvements allowed many Sikh males to sponsor family members, reuniting families after many years of separation.

The so-called twice migrants were Sikhs who first settled in East Africa as indentured laborers to build the Kenya-Uganda railway during the early 1900s and were subsequently expelled under systematic Africanization policies in Kenya (1968) and Uganda (1972). Most East African Sikhs arrived in Britain as political refugees. Many of these two-time immigrants were skilled laborers with capital acquired in East Africa. They also brought with them community-building skills, which helped them quickly orient and resettle in Britain. The myth of return characterizing many of their Punjabi countrymen did not apply to them, given the lack of a strong attachment to India and, perhaps more important, because they arrived as complete family units, unlike the majority of Sikhs. An additional important difference is the absence of the traditional controlling influences by kinship groups and village ties in Punjab. These influences are much stronger among those Sikhs who migrated directly to Britain, affecting all aspects of their identity, customs, and practices.

Whereas the majority of these secondary migrants were of the Ramgarhia caste, a middle-caste grouping among the Sikhs of Punjab, the skill sets they brought with them from Africa allowed them to move quickly into higher class positions, an important factor in class-conscious Britain. Most of their Jat counterparts, on the other hand, arrived in the United Kingdom as unskilled workers. Moreover, since in East Africa Ramgarhias were the dominant caste, most Sikhs in Uganda or Kenya gave caste little significance as a defining identity marker. In Britain, however, despite their economic successes, they were subjected to traditional caste discrimination by their Sikh compatriots, attributable mainly to attitudes of superiority on the part of the dominant Jat caste; for Jats, caste remains perhaps the most powerful organizing principle. This has led to considerable internal strife within Britain's Sikh community, characterized by caste-oriented *gurdwaras* and associations and closely maintained endogamous marriage practices.

In white-dominated British society, however, as a result of racism and simply a lack of awareness of these differences, Sikhs have tended to be perceived as a highly homogeneous group. There are signs of changing attitudes toward caste, however, especially among younger Sikhs, be they from the dominant Jat caste, Khatris, Ramgarhias, or others. There are calls for a more inclusive identity as British Sikhs, a change that has already and will continue to serve the community in terms of collective action and political mobilization for the good of all Sikhs.

The last important wave of Sikhs came as a result of the political turmoil in Punjab in the 1980s. The clashes and violence led hundreds of Sikhs to seek refuge in the United Kingdom. While only a few were actually granted asylum, the government allowed more than two thousand Sikhs to stay. These tragic events, perhaps more than anything else, have led to a more united Sikh identity and consciousness, despite caste and class divisions. All Sikhs, regardless of their affiliations or views, were branded as terrorists. This derogatory identifier, imposed on Sikhs mainly by the media, has prompted Sikhs to more boldly assert their ethnic and religious identity. Following the events of 1984, more Sikhs began wearing turbans and showing a stronger consciousness of their Sikh roots, beliefs, and cultural practices.

THE BHANGRA PHENOMENON

Bhangra music and dance, considered by many as the quintessential Punjabi cultural marker, has become a significant feature of the Sikh diasporic identity. It began in the United Kingdom but has spread to other important centers of the diaspora. In its traditional form, Bhangra refers to a male peasant dance performed to the beat of drums in celebration of the wheat harvest and the traditional Baisakhi festival in regions of East and West Punjab. The loud beat of the drums accentuates the vigorous body movements of the male dancers; Bhangra represents for Punjabis all that is celebratory and joyful.

With the division of India, Bhangra assumed a new role as a symbol of essential Punjabiyat (Punjabi identity, or "Punjabness"). Bhangra thus was transformed from a localized dance form to an icon, a crucial representation of the turmoil and displacement suffered in the wake of the partition. The government of Punjab, educational facilities, and rural associations began sponsoring special Bhangra performances and competitions. The dance itself was changed with the addition of movements from other traditions and of new instruments and singing styles.

Sikh migrants to Britain in the post–World War II period brought Bhangra with them, where it continued to develop its iconic role yet now in these new communities. It became a key element at Sikh birthday parties, weddings, and other community celebrations. The first British Bhangra recording group was Alaap, founded in 1977 in Southall, soon followed by other groups after Alaap's initial success. During the 1980s Bhangra music also responded to the traumatic events taking place in the homeland, leading to new perceptions of "place" and "displacement." In addition, in the 1980s and 1990s Bhangra fused with other forms of music and instrumentation, especially Western instruments as well as other cultural forms such as hip-hop, reggae, and rap. With these fusions, a new form of urban music, "British Bhangra," reached new audiences and incorporated new themes and ideas. Bhangra has also moved from its traditional and exclusively male-oriented base to include female artists and DJs, adding new interpretations, movements, and sounds and an easy mixing of genders in nightclubs featuring Bhangra music.

For many, these songs express the anger and suffering of those marginalized from the dominant culture by the forces of discrimination. Bhangra has also allowed for the articulation of difference, the fusion of cultural styles, and, perhaps most important, a challenge to notions of Britishness and what constitutes British identity. More-over, beyond traditional concerns with the homeland and displace-ment, Bhangra artists have also tackled internal divisions and prej-udices, including gender inequality and caste. Also of note, the diasporic Bhangra phenomenon, initially based in Britain but today found in major centers worldwide, has also spread to the homeland of Punjab and other places throughout India.

Though Bhangra has no direct ties to the Sikh religion, it has the vital function of articulating and projecting Sikh and Punjabi culture and identity. Through dance and music the story of place has been celebrated while narratives of exile lament the forces of displacement. And while not a strictly Sikh tradition, Bhangra as representative of the Punjabi Jat sense of Punjabiyat has been closely tied to the trajec-tory of Sikh identity. As such it serves as a unifying force between Sikhs of Punjab and Sikhs of the diaspora. Bhangra, as the essential male Punjabi Jat dance and, by association, the essential male Pun-jabi Jat Sikh dance, has, according to some scholars, done a great deal to reinforce a hypermasculine projection of both Punjabi culture and the Sikh religion.

Bhangra has moreover become a crossover hit in Europe, Austra-lia, North America, and beyond. This successful intersection of the mainstream and the marginal, the popular and traditional added to the richness of global culture and interaction. Others argue, how-ever, that the great tradition of Bhangra is in peril because of its rapid move away from its rural, male, localized roots and that it is taking on a Westernized character antithetical to its "true" Punjabi nature. What was once promoted as an ideal counter to Sikh youth's adapta-tion to harmful Western ways is perceived by some as a new wave of irreligiousness creeping into the Sikh community.

Attempts are being made to minimize Bhangra's connection to Sikhism, stressing its roots in Punjabi *culture* instead. This argument has been countered with an insistence that Sikhs generally do not make rigid distinctions between the religious and nonreligious, or religious and political, the latter clearly evident in *gurdwara* politics today. Bhangra for many continues to be an important way to express Sikh heritage and identity.

Sikhs in Canada

Most major urban centers in Canada have evidence of Sikhs; turbans and colorful Punjabi clothing known as *salwar kameez* (loose-fitting trousers and long tunic) are increasingly recognizable in cities and towns across Canada. Delicious Punjabi cuisine, known for its liberal use of clarified butter and cream, is available in most cities. Sikh *gurdwaras* have become common across the Canadian landscape.

According to the 2001 census, there are about three hundred thousand Sikhs in Canada. The actual number is likely significantly higher, some projecting there may be closer to four hundred thousand Sikhs in Canada today. It is believed that the earliest presence of Sikhs in Canada was in 1897 when the Sikh Lancers and Infantry regiment visited Vancouver after celebrating Queen Victoria's Diamond Jubilee. In celebration of the centennial of the Sikh arrival in Canada, pins, T-shirts, and traditional Punjabi outfits could be seen sporting an intertwined symbol of the *khanda* and the Canadian maple leaf honoring Sikh contributions to Canadian society.

SIKH PATTERNS OF MIGRATION TO CANADA

In 1904 a group of about thirty Punjabi immigrants arrived in Canada to work in the lumber industry in British Columbia. Although the majority of the new immigrants were Sikhs from Punjab, they were falsely identified as "Hindoos," the name used to identify all immigrants of Indian origin. It should also be said, however, that Punjabi Sikhs at the beginning of the twentieth century were not nearly as concerned with clear-cut distinctions between Sikhs and Hindus as many Sikhs were in later years. During the first decade of the twentieth century, about 5,000 Indian men, mostly Sikhs, entered Canada. These immigrants faced serious discrimination during the early years after their arrival. They were restricted in terms of their involvement in the military and the right to vote; even access to housing, education, and other public services was limited. Canada was a "white man's country," official government policies and less obvious discriminatory attitudes effectively discouraging nonwhite individuals from calling Canada home. By 1911 a number of South Asians had returned to India or moved to California, where a larger group of Indian immigrants lived, leaving a decreased presence in Canada of 2,315. By 1921 the total number of Indian immigrants in Canada was at 1,016.

One effective restriction put in place by the Canadian government was a law passed in 1908 requiring all immigrants into Canada to have traveled on a "continuous journey" from their country of origin. This effectively ended entry from India since few ships were capable of continuous travel from India to a Canadian port. The policy had a direct effect on the passengers on the *Komagata Maru,* which arrived in Vancouver from Hong Kong with over three hundred hopeful immigrants, most of them Sikhs. Despite the ship's nonstop journey from Hong Kong, the ship's passengers were refused entry into Canada because their journey did not start in India. After sitting at anchor in Vancouver for more than two months, the ship eventually had to return its passengers to India. This incident is held up today as indicative of Canada's racist and exclusionary policies near the turn of the century.

After this incident, stung by Canada's implicit support from the British government, a number of Sikhs in Canada and the United States became, between 1913 and 1917, involved in anti-British revolutionary activity known as *ghadar* (mutiny). The activity consisted mainly in the collection of funds for an Indian revolution against the British. When war against Germany broke out in 1914, activist Indians left Canada to fight against Britain in India. The rebellion nonetheless failed.

Most early Sikh immigrants were males who had left their families behind in Punjab. The 1911 census shows that there were only three South Asian women of a total of about two thousand men. These initial immigrants often sponsored other male relatives in a pattern of chain migration. Given the overt discrimination toward them by their fellow Canadians and their deeply held cultural and religious values that discouraged marriage outside their ethnic and religious identities, few Sikhs intermarried within the broader Canadian society. In this regard, Canada's Sikhs differed from Sikhs who had immigrated to the United States, especially agricultural areas in California where a large number of early Sikh immigrants married Mexican-American women. These mixed families quickly established themselves in their new homeland on their own farms. Most Canadian Sikhs, on the other hand, saw themselves as settling in Canada for the short term and, upon acquiring sufficient wealth, returning to India. Eventually, however, a number of early Sikh male migrants brought their wives and children to Canada with them and thought less of a permanent return to Punjab as opportunities grew in their new country of residence.

After World War II and India's independence in 1947, Canada's doors once again opened to Indian immigrants. With new policies in place for selecting newcomers based on their level of education and job qualifications, different classes of South Asians began arriving in Canada. While these policy changes applied to all immigrants from India, the Sikhs figured prominently among the newcomers. Unlike the earliest Sikh laborers, who settled in small towns offering agricultural and forestry job opportunities in British Columbia, this new wave of immigrants was largely urban professionals who settled in the major cities, Toronto and Montreal in particular. Nonetheless, similar patterns of chain migration along kinship networks continued among the Sikh immigrants.

The latest wave of Sikh immigration to Canada took place in the 1980s and 1990s with the deepening conflict between the Indian government and a small number of Sikh separatists intent on establishing the sovereign Sikh state of Khalistan. Terrible violence resulted, especially after the storming of the Golden Temple in Amritsar by the Indian Army and the revenge killing of Indira Gandhi by her Sikh bodyguards. Many Sikhs, including some separatists, sought refuge in Canada.

GURDWARAS IN CANADA

The year 1904 also marked the first appearance in Canada of the Guru Granth Sahib, brought to a private home in Port Moody, British Columbia. The first *gurdwara* built in Canada was the Vancouver Sikh Temple, established in 1908; by 1920 there were seven other *gurdwaras* in British Columbia. The number of *gurdwaras* in the country increases yearly, not only in major cities but also in small rural settlements. Although there have been attempts to bring all Canadian *gurdwaras* under a single national religious administration, *gurdwaras* throughout Canada operate as independent entities controlled and managed by an elected executive board in each *gurdwara*.

In the face of the discrimination the early Sikhs experienced upon arrival in Canada, many of the earliest Sikh immigrants had made attempts to blend into Canadian society. Many replaced traditional Punjabi clothes with Western attire and cut their hair. With the arrival of new immigrants after World War II, many of these adaptations were challenged. The 1950s witnessed the first split in the Canadian Sikh community. While most *gurdwaras* included clean-shaven Sikhs, some members began to argue that *gurdwara* management committees should be restricted to Sikhs following the Khalsa form. Other *gurdwaras* allowed clean-shaven Sikhs to serve as elected officials. These divisions intensified with the heavy immigration of the late 1960s and 1970s. Many of the new immigrants from India were strict observers of keeping the hair uncut who viewed the practices of the earlier Sikh immigrants as far too lax. For example, many Sikhs entered the *gurdwara* bareheaded, something considered highly disrespectful in India. Many of the Sikhs entering Canada during the time of Punjab disturbances in the 1980s brought with them their political ideals and dreams of a separate state of Khalistan. Conflicts between Sikhs became more and more tense, especially in Vancouver, at times breaking into violence. Clashes between pro- and anti-Khalistan Sikhs occurred in the *gurdwaras*, still major sites of political wrangling between the two groups.

One result of these political battles has been a reexamination of Sikh identity. These same issues divide Sikhs today. As we have seen, Sikh identity is not uniform but encompasses numerous identities. For the most part, Sikhs are content to live with diverse understandings of what it means to be a Sikh. However, since the 1980s, issues of identity have rested on perceived differences between "observant Sikhs" and "unobservant Sikhs." Many Sikhs who see themselves as observant reject this characterization of the different views of Sikh identity.

The Canadian media focused on the confrontations between opposing Sikh groups, and from this negative publicity the Sikhs in Canada became less known for their spiritual practices than for the political battles being waged in the *gurdwaras* by a small minority of the Sikh community. One such well-publicized dispute broke out in the late 1990s. For five hundred years, Sikhs in India have sat on the floor for the communal meal *(langar)* after their religious services. Sikhs believe this communal eating demonstrates what is at the heart of Sikhism, equality among all regardless of caste, gender, or class. This tenet is particularly important in Indian society, where caste rules prohibit certain groups sharing food with others. However, in a small number of Canadian *gurdwaras,* chairs and tables are used for sharing the meal. This has proved a point of great contention between Sikhs who insist all must sit in neat rows on the floor, as the early gurus instructed, and those who maintain using tables and chairs in no way goes against their teachings and is simply a practical adaptation to the exigencies of their new homeland.

SIKHS AND THE COURTS IN CANADA

Many legal battles have been fought in the Canadian courts to allow Khalsa Sikhs to maintain their Sikh identity markers. Following Indian precedents, in 1986 the Toronto police department began to allow Sikh officers to wear their turbans as part of their uniform. Another important case involved a Sikh officer in the Royal Canadian Mounted Police (RCMP). The debate as to whether he should be allowed to wear a turban was at times highly charged. Some Canadians felt that religious rights should not supersede the time-honored, distinctive headdress of the RCMP. However, the Canadian courts deemed the religious rights of a Sikh RCMP officer as overriding any historic and cultural norms. Thus, in 1991, Baltej Singh Dhillon became the first Sikh officer in Canada to proudly serve his country in the blue and red colors of the RCMP, crowned by his turban. Other cases have involved Sikh children being prohibited from wearing the Sikh dagger *(kirpan)* on school grounds. Many non-Sikhs have claimed the dagger is essentially a weapon and not a religious object, the claim made especially in cases where a student wears a relatively long version of the insignia. In 1990 the Ontario Human Rights Commission ruled that while Sikh students and teachers could wear the dagger, it had to be securely fastened inside their clothing and could not be longer than seven inches. The Supreme Court of Canada in 2006 overruled a Montreal school board's forbidding a Sikh student from wearing his dagger to school. In its ruling, the court did establish the condition that the dagger has to be sheathed and worn underneath clothing.

Part of the problem is that although many Sikhs feel that a small symbol worn as a pin or on a necklace suffices, others carry an actual dagger with a cutting edge. Still others believe that only a full-sized sword fulfills the requirements of the five *k*s as ordained by Guru Gobind Singh. Similar court cases involving Sikh rights have taken place throughout the Sikh diaspora.

Sikhs in the United States

It is estimated that there are about two hundred thousand Sikhs in the United States, though a precise figure is unavailable since Sikhs have thus far been counted within the larger category of Asian Indians. It is likely, however, that Sikhs will be counted separately in the next census, allowing for a more accurate picture of their presence in the United States.

The first American Sikh *gurdwara,* built in Stockton, California, in 1915, served as a combination sacred space, employment information center, political forum, dining hall, and meeting place where Punjabi customs and language could be shared. It remained an important hub of Sikh life until the 1970s and was the only major Sikh center until 1947. Beginning in the late 1940s *gurdwaras* began to be built in other parts of the country.

Highly publicized controversies surrounding Khalistan, issues of identity, and *gurdwara* politics have also figured in Sikh communities in the United States. In 1971, Jagjit Singh Chauhan, living in Britain and the self-proclaimed spokesperson for the creation of Khalistan, visited the United States and placed an advertisement in the *New York Times* proclaiming the formation of Khalistan. He collected millions of dollars for its establishment, a significant portion of it coming from the United States.

The 1984 attack on the Golden Temple and assassination of Indira Gandhi affected Sikhs in the United States as in other countries of the diaspora. This led, in some cases, to conflict and estrangement of Sikhs from other Indian groups in America. Moreover, Sikhs supporting the movement for an independent homeland were frequently branded as terrorists by the media.

PATTERNS OF MIGRATION TO THE UNITED STATES

The history of the Sikhs in the United States is similar to that of the Sikhs in Canada, but it offers interesting differences as well. Sikh immigration to the United States occurred in two phases, the first between 1900 and 1965 and the second, post-1965. The first South Asian immigrants to the United States were mainly Punjabi Sikh males. Between 1904 and 1911 roughly six thousand Sikh men entered the country. Because of the severely limited marriage possibilities, many of these Punjabi men married Mexican women, who shared with the men a similar socioeconomic status and were found acceptable in other ways.

The early years were difficult, marked by overt racism and even riots. The Bellingham (Washington) Riots of 1907 began with white labor leaders demanding the expulsion from the city of all South Asians working in the nearby lumber mills. Leaders feared the newcomers would deprive whites of employment and drive wages down. The immigrants were forced from their bunkhouses and had their property confiscated, and some were jailed while others fled across the border to Canada. In 1910, Los Angeles barred "Hindus" from purchasing homes, and the 1913 Alien Land Law, signed by California and fourteen other states, excluded noncitizens from owning or leasing land. Between 1915 and 1929 about sixteen hundred more immigrants arrived, with just under two hundred arriving up until World War II.

THE GHADAR MOVEMENT

Before World War II, about sixty-five hundred South Asians were deported or left voluntarily within the first two decades of immigration. Many who left did so to take part in anti-British revolutionary activities, such as the Ghadar (Revolution) movement. Har Dayal, a Hindu student at Oxford University, had declined his scholarship in protest against the British educational system in India. He arrived in California and, along with other leaders, organized the Ghadar Party, establishing a weekly newspaper of the same name in 1913. Though the party leaders were mainly Hindus, the majority of party members were rural Sikhs, who were also largely responsible for financing the movement. Meetings and rallies were held throughout California, calling on Sikhs to support the revolutionary cause.

In his writings and speeches, Dayal and other leaders urged all Indians to return to India to fight for the overthrow of the British. The *Komagata Maru* incident in Vancouver in 1914 was used to mobilize the rising discontent among South Asians in North America stemming from racial discrimination and oppression. Ghadarites seized on the outbreak of World War I as an opportune time to launch their revolutionary activities in India. Hundreds of Sikhs returned to India, only to face arrest or the realization that their revolutionary schemes were simply not feasible. The British government pressured officials in Washington to curtail Ghadar activities, and a number of arrests were made, both in India and in America. By 1917 the Ghadar movement in America had collapsed.

U.S. V. BHAGAT SINGH THIND

In 1923 the famous *U.S. v. Bhagat Singh Thind* decision of the Supreme Court ended immigration from what were known as the Asiatic zones, including India, Burma, and Thailand (Siam). Not only were new immigrants not allowed into the United States but also immigrants who had already arrived on American soil were barred from returning to their native countries because they would not be permitted reentry. This also made it impossible to sponsor family members in coming to America. The Supreme Court's decision allowed for the possibility that immigrants from these zones could have their citizenship revoked, thus rendering them stateless and precluding noncitizens from attaining citizenship; the decision and its unjust consequences hung over Sikhs and others in this category until after World War II.

1948–1965

From 1948 to 1965, a new quota system allowed small numbers of immigrants from India, and the numbers remained low, around five thousand new arrivals. And new laws allowed for families to be reunited, home-country visitation rights, and the securing of spouses from India. Eventually the right to vote and full protection under U.S. law were granted. The quota system was terminated in 1965, which resulted in large-scale immigration for the first time since the early 1900s.

The majority of early Sikh immigrants were agriculturists who settled on the West Coast. By 1920, many had become farm operators, leasing farmland averaging forty acres on a share or cash basis. As the laws barring immigration and the purchase of land went out of force, more family members were sponsored for immigration and offered employment on family farms. Today, the Sikhs of Yuba and Sutter counties in California represent the largest Sikh agricultural population outside India. The professional class of Sikhs who arrived after 1965 headed to larger urban centers, where they acquired jobs as engineers, doctors, and specialists in information technology.

SIKHS AND 9/11

The events of 9/11 ushered in a new era for Sikhs in North America. In the United States, the first casualty of the anti-Muslim sentiment that swept across the country was a Sikh, mistakenly identified as a follower of Osama bin Laden because of his turban. A new form of discrimination and such incidents continue to plague Sikhs in the United States. Many Sikhs have been forced to wake to the fact they are part of a racial and religious minority and not seen as "real Americans."

In response to the backlash, however, the community began a successful campaign to educate the public about Sikhism. A number of online groups have been formed that serve as databases on all matters Sikh, history, religion, and culture. There are also watchdog groups that keep track of abuses against Sikhs in the United States and North America and also in Europe and Asia. These groups include the United Sikhs, Sikh Coalition, Sikh Council on Religion and Education, and the Sikh Human Rights Group.

CHAPTER 6

Sikh Diversity

There have been differences in Sikh identity and Sikh loyalties since the time of the living gurus. Although the Khalsa Sikh identity has often been presented as normative and the only authentic expression of what constitutes Sikh identity, there is no such consensus in this regard among Sikhs. The term "sect" is often applied to Sikhs outside mainstream Sikhism, but the term is viewed pejoratively by such Sikhs. Labels such as "orthodox" and "nonorthodox" are also problematic given their association with Judaism and Christianity. It is perhaps most reasonable to think in terms of there existing a variety of groups within Sikhism.

Differences in the Sikh community existed from the very beginning of the Sikh tradition. As a result of Guru Nanak's establishing succession based on merit as opposed to lineage, a number of the gurus' sons created their own followings. One such group is the ascetic Udasi order, who claim to trace their authority to Guru Nanak's eldest son, Srichand. Another guru's son established a following whose members came to be called Minas.

Namdhari and Nirankari Sikhs

Two groups that have important present-day roles in Sikhism are the Nirankari and Namdhari Sikhs. These groups began as Sikh reform movements in the mid-nineteenth century, antecedents to the Singh Sabha reformers of the late nineteenth century. The Nirankaris were followers of Baba Dayal (1783–1855), a reformer critical of many of the practices followed by Sikhs after the time of Maharajah Ranjit Singh. As the name Nirankar (Formless One) suggests, Nirankaris hold the formlessness of the Divine as a central belief. Baba Dayal believed that Sikhs had lost their moorings of the central discipline of *nam simran* and were too intent on acquiring political stature and wealth. Focusing on the message of liberation preached by the early gurus, Baba Dayal's message did not include the later emphasis on the Khalsa order and the five *k*s introduced by Guru Gobind Singh. However, some of the reforms introduced by the Nirankaris, such as the circling of the Guru Granth Sahib during the wedding ritual as opposed to the sacred fire of the Hindus, have been assimilated into mainstream Sikhism. Another important though divisive distinction of the Nirankaris is their belief in the need for a living guru to guide them, one from a living guru lineage (beyond that of the ten gurus), a lineage that continues to the present time through Baba Dayal's successors. For many Sikhs, this understanding is sacrilegious and contradictory to Guru Gobind Singh's establishment of the Guru Granth Sahib as the final, sole, and eternal guru of the Sikhs.

Nirankari Sikhs should not to be confused with another group, the Sant Nirankaris, an offshoot of the original group. Sant Nirankaris have adopted writings by their leaders as supreme, alongside the Guru Granth Sahib. In 1978 a violent clash took place between Sant Nirankaris and a group called the Akhand Kirtani Jatha related to what the latter group perceived as an increasing irreverence for the Guru Granth Sahib and anti-Sikh teaching by the Sant Nirankaris. More violence between the two groups followed, and the Sant Nirankaris continue to be viewed with a great deal of antipathy by mainstream Sikhs.

The Namdharis have had an important historical role in Sikhism. They were active in the struggle against British rule in India. They foreshadowed a number of the initiatives of Mohandas Gandhi, including the traditionally made Indian cloth and rejection of such British institutions as the postal system. Namdharis set up their own elaborate communication network.

Another name for the Namdharis is Kuka Sikhs, *kuk* meaning "shriek," relating to their loud cries during some of their rituals. The name Namdhari reflects their particular emphasis on the constant repetition of the divine name. They differ from the Nirankaris in their belief that their guru lineage has continued in an unbroken line from the time of Guru Gobind Singh, denying that he died in 1708; rather, he remained alive, living anonymously, then passed the mantle on to Balak Singh, the founder of the Namdharis. Unlike the Nirankaris, Namdharis wholeheartedly embrace the Khalsa ideal started by Guru Gobind Singh. They consider, however, their interpretation of the Khalsa ideal to be a pure one, reflected in the Namdhari code of conduct.

Namdharis are easily recognizable by their all-white Punjabi clothing. They are also strict vegetarians and strongly opposed to alcohol consumption, which additionally sets them apart from mainstream Sikhs. In addition, marriage is solemnized by circumambulating fire. In this they conform to Sikh marriage practices predating the reforms of the early twentieth century. Ceremonies are also often conducted for multiple couples for economic reasons. Namdharis believe that dowries are at the core of misogynist attitudes toward women and must be thoroughly done away with. Multiple marriage practices are thus also a way Namdharis ensure that dowries are not provided by the parents of brides. Another important contribution of the Namdharis has been their insistence that both men and women be initiated into the Khalsa order, virtually unheard of in the mainstream Sikh community before the twentieth century.

Namdharis have historically been dominated by members of the Ramgarhia caste, a relatively low-ranking caste in the hierarchy of northern India. In this way they also differ from the Nirankaris, whose constituents have historically come from primarily urban and upper-caste groups.

Nihangs

Although Nihangs are relatively few in number, they have long viewed themselves as the true representatives of the Khalsa order. Under Maharajah Ranjit Singh, they were renowned for their bravery on the battlefield. Today, many Nihangs remain unmarried and devote themselves to the running of distinctive Nihang camps. They are conspicuous in being heavily armed with a range of steel weapons, wearing only blue Punjabi clothing, and sporting unusually

A young Nihang, UK. Courtesy of Kamalroop Singh.

high turbans. Historically, Nihangs consumed cannabis to fortify themselves before battle, and its consumption continues today.

Nanaksar Sikhs

Nanaksar Sikhs originated through the teachings of Nand Singh (1869?–1943) and subsequently developed into a well-defined group with practices that are distinct from those of mainstream Sikhs. Even more so than in traditional *gurdwaras,* the Guru Granth Sahib is treated with utmost devotion. Scripture is understood as an actual person with real physical needs. For example, during the winter months the Guru Granth Sahib is covered with additional cloth to ensure sufficient warmth. This practice stems from Nand Singh's mystical experience in which Guru Nanak physically appeared to him from out of the Guru Granth Sahib.

Nanaksar Sikhs are strict vegetarians and lean toward asceticism as the ideal way of life. Leaders have generally been celibate, as are those serving in the *gurdwaras*. Nanaksar *gurdwaras* do not fly the saffron flag of the Khalsa order. Today there are several splinter groups operating under the Nanaksar umbrella.

Akand Kirtani Jatha

The Akhand Kirtani Jatha is a group that developed under the leadership of a pious Sikh named Bhai Randhir Singh (1878–1961). Akhand Kirtani Jatha Sikhs are known for their rigorousness in the Khalsa discipline and their strict vegetarianism. They also practice unique forms of communal singing, particularly its all-night performance. Another feature of the group is their disciplined and rapid repetition of the name Vahiguru.

Perhaps most distinctive, Akhand Kirtani Jatha Sikhs believe that naturally growing hair is not part of the symbolism of the Khalsa order, their five *k*s including instead a small turban. Furthermore, both women and men must wear turbans. Members of this group also follow a particular Khalsa discipline described in their own code of conduct.

Sikh Dharma of the Western Hemisphere / 3HO Sikhs

In the 1960s, a Punjabi Sikh customs official, Harbhajan Singh Puri (1929–2004), arrived in California after initially settling in Canada. Within a few years he had changed his name to Yogi Bhajan and founded an ashram for his organization, the 3HO (Healthy, Happy, Holy Organization). His followers were almost exclusively white, middle-class counterculture seekers longing for insight into the ancient spiritual wisdom of India.

Yogi Bhajan offered his students a unique blend of Eastern and Western ideas and lifestyles, especially focused on Kundalini yoga and healthy living practices. He taught that through a rigorous routine of meditation, dormant energy *(kundalini)* resting at the base of the spine could ascend through centers called chakras. Upon reaching the top of the head, these energies would climax and allow for inner union with divinity.

Devotees were called yogis and yoginis. At its inception 3HO had little connection to Sikhism. This changed in 1971, when Yogi Bhajan took a number of his followers to Harimandir Sahib, where he introduced Sikh tenets into his teachings. After 1973 the group was known as the Sikh Dharma of the Western Hemisphere, and Yogi Bhajan changed his name to Siri Singh Sahib Bhai Sahib Harbhajan Singh Khalsa Yogiji.

Today, members perceive themselves as full-fledged converts to Sikhism and strictly follow the Sikh Reht Maryada, despite differing in significant ways from mainstream Sikhism. All members adopt the name Khalsa joined with more traditional Sikh names, and both men and women wear white Punjabi clothes and white turbans. The group continues to focus on Kundalini yoga practices along with their devotion to the Guru Granth Sahib and *nam simran* meditation. They are also unique in receiving ordination as 3HO ministers. As noted, there is no ordained or trained ministry in traditional Sikhism.

For the most part, adherents of the Sikh Dharma of the Western Hemisphere and Punjabi Sikhs rarely congregate together. Marriage between members of the groups is virtually nonexistent. Although members of the Sikh Dharma of the Western Hemisphere increasingly learn the Punjabi language, they also include, unlike in the majority of Punjabi Sikh *gurdwaras,* the English language in the music and sermons in their services.

These Sikh converts have assumed an important role in stressing Sikhism's egalitarian core, insisting that men and women must play equal parts in all aspects of Sikh religious life. In this regard the group is highly critical of traditional Punjabi Sikh culture and religious practices. They are firm in their belief that Punjabi Sikhs have not lived up to the standards set by the Sikh gurus with regard to gender and caste discrimination.

In the late 1990s, a group of Sikh converts insisted on being allowed to take part in rituals at Harimandir Sahib, rituals that have never been open to Punjabi Sikh women. This incident, along with the 3HO custom of women as the five beloved ones in *gurdwaras* run by the Sikh Dharma of the Western Hemisphere, has raised questions about the egalitarian claims of mainstream Sikhs.

Although the group has remained small, comprising perhaps a few thousand adherents, it exerts a significant influence on Sikhism in the West, particularly in the United States and Canada. They can best be understood as fitting within the rubric of a Sikh new religious movement, given their melding of Eastern and Western views and practices. A number of 3HO musicians have won accolades, especially among New Age audiences. Some 3HO yoga instructors in the Los Angeles area have become personal trainers and yoga instructors to Hollywood's elite. In addition, 3HO has become a potent economic force through a number of the organization's enterprises, including Khalsa International Industries and Trades, which focuses on health foods and teas, and Akal Securities, one of the largest private security companies in North America.

Yogi Bhajan died in 2004, and it remains to be seen which direction 3HO will take without his charismatic leadership. The Sikh Dharma of the Western Hemisphere is currently headed by a group of 3HO ministers known as the Khalsa Council.

CHAPTER 7

Conclusion: Sikhs in the Twenty-first Century

Sikhism in the twenty-first century is entering a new era that promises to be both challenging and rewarding. In terms of numbers, Sikhism has now replaced Judaism as the fifth largest religion worldwide. The regional character of Sikhism is being altered by characteristic migration patterns of Sikhs worldwide. This has led to greater attention given to the possible effects on the tradition of global economics, politics, and religion. New cultural, diasporic, anthropological, and religious studies are emerging based on a renewed interest in Sikhism.

Politically and economically, the Sikhs of Punjab are attempting to find ways to fit within the parameters of the modern state and present-day realities of the age of globalization while struggling to define and establish their own political interests as the majority population in Punjab. The vast numbers of Sikhs who have migrated elsewhere have had positive economic influences on the homeland and their kin through remittances to Punjab. Many have also donated significant funds for the upkeep of important shrines and *gurdwaras* in ancestral villages. At the same time, Punjab has lost many of its best and brightest to new homelands, many with no intention of returning to take up residence in India.

Sikhs continue to face their extreme minority status within India's overwhelming Hindu majority, struggling to keep their distinct religious identity intact while recognizing the need to work and interact peaceably with the larger religious communities in India. The issue of Sikh identity continues to confront the community given the diversity of Sikh practices and forms of devotion, including devotion to living saints and gurus by large numbers of adherents. Clashes between members of the Sikh mainstream and Sikhs who follow other spiritual teachers appear regularly in the media. Some of these clashes appear to be caste based.

At the same time many youth, in India and in the diaspora, reject such Sikh identity markers as uncut hair and turbans. Sikh leaders are attempting to reach their youth in ways that honor Sikhism's timeless truths while acknowledging that generational differences and needs are making these truths increasingly difficult to communicate.

Sikhs and the Internet

Scholars of religion are giving more attention to the significance of the Internet in the study of religion. Sikhs, along with other religious communities, have embraced this technology and are using it as a learning tool and resource. The ways that Sikhism and the Internet are intersecting are many. Moreover, the number of Sikh sites appears to be growing almost daily. Hymns and verses of the Guru Granth Sahib can be found through using search engines; examples of common Sikh baby names can be found online. Cyber courses teach the writing of the Gurmukhi script and offer effective tools for learning the Punjabi language. Sikh musical modes can be learned online, and tips can be found on playing the harmonium or other instruments associated with Sikh worship. Aspects of Sikh history or specific Sikh tenets are easy to find for discussion and debate between interested parties. Sikhs make extensive use of YouTube and other video- or audio-sharing sites to broadcast hymns, share turban-tying techniques, and publicize Sikh martial arts competitions. Maps pinpointing ancestral villages can be posted, and it's possible for family members in rural Punjab to stay in daily touch with loved ones in cities in Canada and elsewhere. Philanthropic ventures in Punjab can be more easily and carefully administered from distant lands via the Internet. The worldwide Sikh community has never in its history been so connected, nor has there ever been as much information so readily available to anyone interested in learning about Sikhism.

One important question of interest to scholars is how the new communications technology is changing religion. With regard to

Sikhism, though many sites simply reproduce information that can be found elsewhere, others are offering new ways of considering various aspects of Sikhism. Western Sikhs in particular are grappling with questions of identity and authority via blogs, discussion forums, videos, and online chat sites. Strategies are being explored in an attempt to claim global legitimacy for what has until recently been perceived as a regional tradition while also aligning Sikh values with dominant secular and humanistic value systems. The emergence of the virtual realm has raised the question of authority—who speaks for Sikhs? The World Wide Web is the ultimate democratic tool for anyone with access to a computer. Anyone can construct or have built a Web site with the aim of disseminating Sikhism if they choose to.

As an example of the possible ramifications of this new reality, I asked students to analyze an essay posted at an online Sikhism site. After a great deal of investigating, students eventually realized that what they had assumed was a scholarly essay had been written by a Sikh teenager for a high school assignment. The young man had managed to create a sleek site purporting to be a Sikh resource. And certainly if one peruses the most popular sites on Sikhism, they are not those of scholars of the Sikh religion. Moreover, they are generally not associated with the traditional authority structures of the Sikhs. Though there are of course official sites of the Shiromani Gurdwara Parbandhak Committee, Harimandir Sahib, the Akal Takht, and various *gurdwaras* around the world, it becomes quickly evident that many of these sites lack the sophistication, reliability, and user-friendliness of those constructed by deeply engaged Sikhs outside the bounds of traditional authority. Also, the majority of the well-maintained sites on Sikhism originate outside India, dominated by Web designers in North America and Britain who perceive their cyberspatial work as a useful service, or *seva* (which is a main tenet of Sikhism), to the Sikh community.

These Web designers have become "new authorities" in Sikhism, not because of their great knowledge of Sikhism but because of their technological expertise. While they bear a genuine devotion to Sikhism, many of these Web creators do not identify themselves as nonspecialists in Sikhism nor make clear they are presenting their version of Sikhism. The Sikh high school student's Web essay is an example of the misunderstandings that can arise in the many cases where the author of a site chooses to keep her or his identity unknown. These new online authorities can exploit the Internet to take on powerful roles as creators and mediators of Sikh knowledge.

Often Sikhism is presented through the liberal and humanistic lenses characteristic of the educational systems of the diaspora in which these Web creators were raised. The practices, values, and attitudes of the vast majority of Sikhs living in rural Punjab are often simply not acknowledged when presenting "the Sikh tradition." Thus, whereas in rural Punjab many Sikhs continue to adhere to a more heterogeneous understanding of Sikhism in their religious views and practices, a far more homogeneous Khalsa identity, similar to that fostered by Singh Sabha reformers, is being furthered by these new online authorities. Issues of representation, namely, *which* particular Sikh identity is being fostered and *who* is speaking for Sikhism, have not been adequately addressed in current research. The need to address this issue only gains in importance as more and more people, particularly students, turn to the Web for information about Sikhism.

Portrayals of Sikhs on the Web reveal that there are forces of homogenization at work. Whereas most Sikhs, even increasingly so in Punjab, cut their hair and no longer wear a turban, an overwhelming majority of pictures of Sikhs posted online show turbaned Sikhs. Even more startling is the frequent image of turbaned Sikh women, despite the fact that few Sikh women wear a turban. Perhaps even more interesting is that many of the most accessible images are of white Sikh women converts of 3HO. Despite this group's miniscule minority among the roughly 23 million Sikhs worldwide, they appear to be playing a significant part in defining Sikhism in the online realm. The ramifications of this tiny, white minority potentially becoming representatives of the Sikh community worldwide are immense and deserve intense scholarly scrutiny.

As mentioned, one important development since 9/11 has been a proliferation of organizations dedicated to protecting Sikh rights. These organizations, many of which have an online presence, operate most effectively in liberal, democratic societies outside India that are built on traditions of the rights of the individual and freedom of religion. Largely by means of the World Wide Web were abuses that Sikhs faced after the tragic events of 9/11 tracked and publicized.

Cyberspace has also become an important religious site for young Sikhs who, perhaps as a result of generational differences or negative *gurdwara* politics, choose not to attend their local *gurdwara*. If for no other reason, many young Sikhs simply cannot understand Punjabi, the language used in *gurdwaras* throughout the diaspora. One appealing feature of the online Sikh congregation is that young people can find there a safe space in which they can anonymously talk about issues related to Sikh identity and religion. Discussions in public online forums also provide non-Sikh parties insights into Sikh internal politics or other matters otherwise not easily gained. Virtual spaces also allow for important discussions of taboo subjects, subjects generally considered out of bounds in many Sikh homes and *gurdwaras*. These include homosexuality, abortion, dating, and, significantly, domestic abuse in Sikh families. Through these discussion forums, young Sikhs in particular are attempting to make sense of perceived clashes between both religious ideals and practices and, for Sikhs in the diaspora, the two cultures they live in, their minority Punjabi culture and the dominant one around them.

The Internet has also become a primary means for arranging marriages. With the click of the mouse, information about a potential spouse can be acquired and a marriage arranged. The possibility for couples to meet and develop relationships online has brought significant changes. Though traditionally meetings were chaperoned by family elders, men and women of marriageable age can now meet freely online. Marriage Web sites catering to the specific needs of the Sikh community have opened the doors to a much larger pool of potential matches, both locally and globally.

There is little indication that these trends will diminish. In fact, numerous reports suggest that online religious activities will only continue to show explosive growth. This leads to important questions such as the Web as sacred space, virtually based spiritual development, and the mystical dimensions of cyberspace. One issue for Sikhs that has not received the attention it deserves is that of Sikh scripture in cyberspace. Considering the reverence offered the text as guru and the rituals associated with maintaining the sanctity of Sikh scripture, the kneeling and bowing before it, ensuring that "the guru" keeps a place above everyday human activity by being placed on a raised platform, and wearing proper head coverings in the presence of the Guru Granth Sahib, the question of how this can be translated into the virtual realm must be addressed. Is being in the presence of the Guru Granth Sahib, the living guru, more important than having virtual access to the words it contains? These and related questions press for consideration at a time when more people than ever before have immediate access to Sikh scripture.

Clearly, the Sikh tradition is facing many of the same issues and questions confronting all religious traditions in the twenty-first century, if none other than the question of how to remain vibrant and relevant in an increasingly globalized and secularized modern world. Historically, Sikhs have shown remarkable resourcefulness in adapting to ever-changing religious, political, and economic pressures, both in the homeland and as migrants in distant lands. The future of Sikhism, though faced with obvious challenges, appears bright. Its innate adaptability will ensure the Sikh community continues to develop and thrive.

Sources Cited and Recommended Readings

Bains, Tara Singh, and Hugh Johnston. *The Four Quarters of the Night: The Life Journey of an Emigrant Sikh*. Montreal: McGill-Queen's University Press, 1995.
- Fascinating glimpse into the life of an early Canadian Sikh.

Cole, W. Owen, and Piara Singh Sambhi. *The Sikhs: Their Religious Beliefs and Practices*. Brighton, UK: Sussex Academic Press, 1995.
- Standard and multifaceted study of the salient features of Sikhism

Ember, M., C. Ember, and I. Skoggard, eds. *Encyclopedia of the Diasporas: Immigrant and Refugee Cultures around the World*. New York: Springer, 2005.
- Comprehensive encyclopedia on immigration and diasporas, including Sikh immigrants to Britain, Africa, Europe, and North America

Grewal, J. S. *The Sikhs of the Punjab*. Cambridge: Cambridge University Press, 1990.
- Classic historical overview of the Sikhs based on both primary and secondary texts

Jakobsh, Doris R. *Relocating Gender in Sikh History: Transformation, Meaning and Identity*. Delhi: Oxford University Press, 2005.
- Examines the process of gender construction among the Sikhs in the context of British colonial rule

———. "Authority in the Virtual Sangat: Sikhism, Ritual and Identity in the Twenty-first Century." *Online: Heidelberg Journal of Religions on the Internet* 2, no. 1 (2006): 24–40. http://www.online.uni-hd.de/.
- Looks at issues of authority and identity in the context of information on Sikhs created for the World Wide Web

Johnston, Hugh. *The Voyage of the Komagata Maru: The Sikh Challenge to Canada's Colour Bar*. Vancouver: University of British Columbia Press, 1989.

- In-depth analysis of the *Komagata Maru* incident in Canada at the turn of the twentieth century

LaBrack, Bruce. *Sikhs of Northern California, 1904–1979.* New York: AMS Press, 1988.

- Comprehensive overview of Sikh history in the United States

MacAuliffe, Max Arthur. *The Sikh Religion: Its Gurus, Sacred Writings and Authors.* 6 vols. Delhi: Low Price Publications, 1996.

- Classic overview of Sikh history and religion, first published 1909. Vol. 1 also available online at http://www.sacred-texts .com/skh/tsr1/index.htm.

McLeod, W. H., ed. and trans. *Textual Sources for the Study of Sikhism.* Chicago: University of Chicago Press, 1984.

- Important study of Sikhism, includes translations of the Adi Granth and Dasam Granth, a number of versions of the Khalsa Reht (Codes of Conduct), and important texts from lesser-known Sikh groups

———. *Who Is a Sikh? The Problem of Sikh Identity.* Oxford: Oxford University Press, 1992.

- Delves into issues of Sikh identity throughout history

———. *Historical Dictionary of Sikhism.* Lanham, MD: Scarecrow Press, 2005.

- Important resource for both students and scholars with an extensive bibliography on Sikhism

Myrvold, Kristina. "Personifying the Sikh Scripture: Ritual Processions of the Guru Granth Sahib in India." In *South Asian Religions on Display: Religious Processions in South Asia and the Diaspora,* edited by Knut A. Jacobsen. London: Routledge, 2008.

- Discusses the centrality of Sikh scripture for Sikhs, particularly its personification as a living guru, and beautifully elucidates the notion of social agency of "text as guru" as well as the cultural habits associated with that personification

Oberoi, Harjot. *The Construction of Religious Boundaries: Culture, Identity and Diversity in the Sikh Tradition.* Delhi: Oxford University Press, 1994.

- Groundbreaking study of the process of Sikh-identity construction in the nineteenth and early twentieth centuries

Shackle, Christopher, and Arvind-Pal Singh Mandair, eds. and
  trans. *Teachings of the Sikh Gurus: Selections from the Sikh Scrip-
  tures.* London: Routledge, 2005.
  • Important study of Sikh scriptures, includes both translations
    of selected segments of scripture and interpretations of as-
    pects of Sikh beliefs as elucidated by scripture
Singh, Gurharpal, and Darshan Singh Tatla. *Sikhs in Britain: The
  Making of a Community.* Delhi: Ajanta Press, 2008.
  • Comprehensive study of the history and process of migration
    and settlement of the Sikhs in Britain
Singh, I. J. *Being and Becoming a Sikh.* Guelph, Ont.: Centennial
  Foundation, 2003.
  • Collection of essays by American I. J. Singh offers insightful
    commentary on aspects of the Sikh devotional and spiritual
    journey, beautifully described through anecdotes from the
    author's life and experiences
Singh, Khushwant. *A History of the Sikhs.* 2 vols. 2nd ed. Delhi,
  Oxford University Press, 1999.
  • Journalist Khushwant Singh offers a very readable examina-
    tion of Sikh history
Singh, Nikky-Guninder Kaur, trans. *The Name of My Beloved:
  Verses of the Sikh Gurus; Devotional Poetry from the Guru Granth
  and the Dasam Granth.* San Francisco: HarperSanFrancisco,
  1995.
  • Offers the only gender-neutral translation of a selection of
    Sikh sacred verses
Singh, Pashaura. *The Guru Granth Sahib: Canon, Meaning and
  Authority.* Delhi: Oxford University Press, 2000.
  • Comprehensive study of Sikh scriptural development by one
    of the foremost scholars in Sikh studies
Takhar, Opinderjit Kaur. *Sikh Identity: An Exploration of Groups
  among Sikhs.* Aldershot, UK: Ashgate, 2005.
  • Important exploration of the history and development of
    groups outside mainstream Sikhism
Vertovic, Steven. "Three Meanings of 'Diaspora,' Exemplified
  among South Asian Religions." *Diaspora* 6, no. 3 (1997): 277–300.

- Offers theoretical formulations pertinent to the Sikhs while also addressing the wider context of South Asian diasporas

INTERNET RESOURCES

British Broadcasting Corporation: http://www.bbc.co.uk/religion/religions/sikhism/
- Excellent, comprehensive site on Sikhism that includes Sikh rituals, beliefs, and Sikhs in the news

Encyclopedia of Canada's People, Sikhs in Canada: http://multiculturalcanada.ca/Encyclopedia/A-Z/s4
- Simon Fraser University's online version of the original encyclopedia created by the Multicultural History Society of Ontario, offers comprehensive history of Canadian Sikhs by Hugh Johnston

Namdhari Sikhs: http://www.namdhari.org/
- Official site of the Namdhari Sikhs and their leader, Satguru Jagjit Singh, includes extensive focus on the historical role of Namdharis during British colonial rule in India

Ontario Consultants on Religious Tolerance: http://www.religioustolerance.org/sikhism.htm
- Focuses on all aspects of religion, including controversies within various religious traditions

PHILTAR: http://philtar.ucsm.ac.uk/encyclopedia/sikhism/index.html
- One of the best scholarly sites on the historical development of Sikhism, including the various strands of premodern and current Sikh groups; based in the University of Cumbria's Department of Religion and Philosophy (PHILTAR: Philosophy, Theology, and Religion)

Punjab Online, Bhangra: http://www.punjabonline.com/servlet/entertain.bhangra
- History, lyrics, and reviews of Bhangra, both traditional and modern forms

Shiromani Gurdwara Parbandhak Committee (SGPC): http://sgpc.net/index-nm.html
- Official site of the SGPC, with links to *kirtan* archives, live audio from Harimandir Sahib, and Sikh publications

Sikhchic: http://www.sikhchic.com/
- Focuses on the religion, art, and culture of the Sikh diaspora

Sikh Coalition: http://www.sikhcoalition.org/
- Site of the well-organized community-based organization active in addressing the legal rights of Sikhs, particularly in the United States; based in Fremont, Calif., and New York City

Sikh Council of Religion and Education (SCORE): http://www.sikhcouncilusa.org/
- Offers a Sikh perspective and voice to educational and interfaith initiatives in the United States

Sikh Foundation: http://www.sikhfoundation.org/
- Focuses on Sikh heritage, culture, and educational initiatives

Sikhism Homepage: http://www.sikhs.org/
- Created in 1994, claims to be the first Web site devoted to Sikhism; includes audio files for download of daily Sikh prayers

Sikh Missionary Society of the U.K.: http://www.gurmat.info/sms/
- Offers wide array of resources focusing on Sikhism

SikhNet: http://www.sikhnet.com/
- Official site of 3HO/Sikh Dharma of the Western Hemisphere, includes online discussion groups and matrimonial and online media links.

Sikh Reht Maryada: http://www.sgpc.net/sikhism/sikh-dharma-manual.html
- English version of this Sikh code of conduct

Simply Bhangra: http://simplybhangra.com/
- Celebrates Bhangra, Urban Desi, and Hindi music; includes news, interviews, downloads, and podcasts from the South Asian music scene

United Sikhs: http://www.unitedsikhs.org/
- Advocates for religious rights of Sikhs worldwide

Index

Page numbers in boldface refer to illustrations.

About the Author

Doris R. Jakobsh, who holds degrees from the University of
Waterloo, Harvard University, and the University of British
Columbia, is an associate professor in the Department of
Religious Studies at the University of Waterloo in Canada. She
has published numerous articles and is the author of *Relocating
Gender in Sikh History: Transformation, Meaning and Identity,*
Delhi (2003), and the editor of *Women in Sikhism: History,
Texts and Experience* (2010). Current projects include editing
a two-volume world religions textbook with a particular focus
on religion in Canada to be published in 2012 as well as a
book on Sikhs and the WWW. Professor Jakobsh is a Steering
Committee Member of the Sikh Consultation of the American
Academy of Religion. She also serves on a number of local
and international editorial boards and advisory committees
associated with the study of religion and Sikh studies.

Production Notes for Jakobsh / SIKHISM

Interior design by Rich Hendel, in 10-point Minion Pro,

with display type in Tarzana Wide.

Composition by Mardee Melton

Printing and binding by Sheridan Books, Inc.

Printed on 55# House White Hi-Bulk D37, 360 ppi